A LOOK AT DERAILMENT TODAY: NORTH AMERICA AND EUROPE

A LOOK AT DERAILMENT TODAY: NORTH AMERICA AND EUROPE

Jean Brittain Leslie
Ellen Van Velsor

Center for Creative Leadership
Greensboro, North Carolina

The Center for Creative Leadership is an international, nonprofit educational institution founded in 1970 to foster leadership and effective management for the good of society overall. As a part of this mission, it publishes books and reports that aim to contribute to a general process of inquiry and understanding in which ideas related to leadership are raised, exchanged, and evaluated. The ideas presented in its publications are those of the author or authors.

The Center thanks you for supporting its work through the purchase of this volume. If you have comments, suggestions, or questions about any Center publication, please contact Walter W. Tornow, Vice President, Research and Publication, at the address given below.

Center for Creative Leadership
Post Office Box 26300
Greensboro, North Carolina 27438-6300

CENTER FOR CREATIVE LEADERSHIP

CCL No. 169

Library of Congress Cataloging-in-Publication Data

Leslie, Jean Brittain.
    A look at derailment today : North America and Europe / Jean Brittain Leslie, Ellen Van Velsor.
        p.   cm.
    Includes bibliographical references.
    ISBN 1-882197-15-1
    1. Executives—United States—Case studies. 2. Career development—United States —Case studies. 3. Management—United States—Case studies. 4. Executives—Europe—Case studies. 5. Career development—Europe—Case studies. 6. Management—Europe—Case studies. I. Van Velsor, Ellen. II. Title.
HD38.25.U6L47 1996
658'.00973—dc20   95-52011
                                                                              CIP

Table of Contents

Acknowledgments

This research project would not have been possible without the support of sponsors and the collaboration of SYMLOG Consulting Group (SCG). (SYMLOG is a registered trademark of the SYMLOG Consulting Group. The SYMLOG-related displays reproduced in this publication are used with permission.)

Several companies joined with the Center for Creative Leadership (CCL) and SCG to form a research consortium. The supporting organizations include: BASF AG, Colgate-Palmolive Company, DHL Worldwide Express, General Electric Company, Warner-Lambert Company, and Wilhelmsen Lines.

Four interviewers—M. Cristina Isolabella (SCG); Angela Stafford, a consultant, in London, England; Bill Shea, former director of the Brussels branch of CCL; and Joan Tavares, former director of programs, CCL, Brussels—traveled throughout Europe to collect interview data. In addition, we are indebted to Kelly Lombardino who helped us contact North American managers for interviews.

Several additional people within CCL helped with the analyses of the case studies. They include John Fleenor, Martha Hughes-James, Cindy McCauley, Sharon Rogolsky, Bill Shea, Sylvester Taylor, and Meena Wilson.

We would also like to acknowledge and thank all of the executives who took the time (from one to three hours) out of their schedules to be interviewed.

Finally, we would like to note that parts of this report have been previously published in *The Academy of Management Executive* and *Healthcare Executive*. We thank those publications for their support.

Introduction

Research studies conducted at the Center for Creative Leadership (CCL) over the past 12 years (Lombardo & McCauley, 1988; McCall & Lombardo, 1983; Morrison, White, & Van Velsor, 1987) have explored the dynamics of derailment among North American executives. Most of these studies have contrasted people who "make it" to the top with those who derail; their purpose has been to understand the kinds of development needed for senior leadership positions. Results from this research have been used in training programs, assessment instruments, and numerous human-resources initiatives in several organizations.

These studies have defined the successful manager as one who has reached at least the general management level and continues to be considered highly promotable by senior executives. The derailed manager is one who, having reached at least the general manager level, either leaves the organization nonvoluntarily (through resignation, being fired, or retiring early) or is plateaued as a result of a perceived lack of fit between personal characteristics and skills and the demands of the job. Derailment is not usually an end to a manager's career. Often, managers who derail in one organization go on to either start their own companies or to be successful in other organizations (Morrison et al., 1987).

CCL's executive derailment research has been useful primarily because it has been a key to understanding the development needed for success in senior leadership positions. Yet as the years go by, researchers as well as human resources professionals have begun to wonder whether derailment factors identified in the United States during the 1980s are standing the test of time and whether they are applicable in other cultures.

One might even go beyond these concerns to wonder whether the concept of derailment remains useful in the context of fast-paced change in organizations and organizational environments. In the face of rapidly downsizing organizations, re-engineering, and the "new employment contract," it may no longer make sense to think about factors related to derailment in a specific organization or at one point in time. Yet in the business world today, the issue of understanding fit between individual skills and characteristics and organizational needs may indeed have become more critical than ever before.

The purpose of this paper is to report on a study that extended CCL's derailment research by comparing contemporary derailed and successful executives in the U.S. and in Europe, and by comparing these results to the earlier findings. Thus we first review CCL's research on executive derailment, then present recent findings for North Americans and Europeans, and finally compare derailment and success themes over time and across cultures. This report is primarily for a research-oriented audience interested in understanding the development needed for senior-level positions.

Summary of CCL Derailment Research in the 1980s

The earliest derailment research, published by McCall and Lombardo in 1983, was based on a set of interviews with senior executives in three U.S. industrial organizations. The interviews yielded a total of 40 case studies, 20 focusing on success and 20 dealing with derailment. This study found that successful executives were identified as high-potential early in their careers, had outstanding track records, were seen as very intelligent and ambitious, and made many sacrifices. Executives who derailed also had run up a string of successes early on and were seen as technical geniuses or tenacious problem-solvers. Yet as they moved up in their organizations and job demands changed, some early strengths became weaknesses and some early weaknesses began to matter. The most common reasons for derailment included specific performance problems, insensitivity to others, failure to delegate or build a team, and overdependence on a single advocate or mentor.

Although the successful and derailed executives shared many of the same skills and flaws, those who had risen to the top: (1) had more diversity in their track records—had done different kinds of things well; (2) maintained composure under stress; (3) handled mistakes with poise and grace; (4) focused on problems and solved them; and (5) got along with all kinds of people.

Later CCL studies expanded on this research in a variety of ways. Morrison et al. (1987) replicated the research but focused on women. In this study, conducted in 25 companies from a wide variety of industries, a total of 22 success factors emerged for executive women, each mentioned by at least two of the senior executives interviewed. Six major success factors were used to describe two-thirds of the successful women: (1) help from above; (2) a track record of achievements; (3) desire to succeed; (4) ability to manage subordinates; (5) willingness to take career risks; and (6) ability to be tough, decisive, and demanding.

Interestingly, help from more senior executives was mentioned by every interviewee as a factor contributing to these women's success. Other top factors (mentioned by over half of the senior executives) attributed to the successful women included intelligence, impressive image, ability to work with others, ability to adapt, and a factor called "easy to be with."

Women who derailed were seen as having good track records of performance early in their careers and as exceptionally intelligent. Some of the more common reasons for derailment among women were an inability to adapt to a boss or culture, performance problems, being overly ambitious, an inability to lead subordinates or to be strategic, presenting a poor image, and poor relationships.

A study by Lombardo and McCauley (1988) expanded on the original research by factor-analyzing a questionnaire derived from the 1983 research but using a database of 355 bosses' ratings of managers. Empirical relationships among the themes were used to collapse the original categories into six scales. In some instances, themes were collapsed into a single category (e.g., "insensitive to others," "cold, aloof, arrogant," "overly ambitious," and "betrayal of trust" into Problems with Interpersonal Relationships). The six derailment factors identified in this study were labeled: Problems with Interpersonal Relationships, Difficulty in Molding a Staff, Difficulty in Making Strategic Transitions, Lack of Follow-through, Overdependence, and Strategic Differences with Management. These factors are encompassed in six derailment scales used in Benchmarks®, a 164-item, multi-rater feedback instrument for the upward appraisal of middle-to-upper-level managers and executives. Benchmarks feedback highlights 16 skills and perspectives that research has shown managers can and must learn in order to be successful, as well as the six derailment scales that can stall a promising career.

Although these studies were carried out by different research teams using different samples of managers at different times, they have at least two things in common. First, each focuses on derailment in a U.S. context. Second, each of these studies is based on data collected more than five years ago. The questions of whether the dynamics of derailment are changing over time or differ for European managers are questions which we now address.

Research Methodology

North American Sample

We interviewed 20 senior executives from 15 Fortune 500 service or manufacturing companies in the United States. The majority of the interviewees (69%) are males in the age range of 49 to 59 years (94%). All of the North American executives interviewed have at least a college degree, with 81% having completed post-university work.

Demographic data on the derailment and success cases were not collected in an effort to conceal identities. General information can, however, be provided from the background information on the case studies. The majority of the derailment (95%) and success (85%) cases are male. Higher education was mentioned as background information in 40% of the derailed cases and 60% of the successful ones. All of the case studies (of both derailment and success) describe senior-level executives.

European Sample

Forty-two English-speaking senior executives from 24 large service or manufacturing organizations located in six European Unity (E.U.) countries (Belgium, France, Germany, Italy, Spain, and the United Kingdom) were interviewed. The European organizations in which we conducted interviews were a mixture of Fortune 500 multinational corporations with major European operations and large indigenous European service or manufacturing organizations. The largest percentage of the European executives interviewed are Spanish (19%). The remainder are Belgian (17%), Italian (17%), French (14%), British (12%), and German (7%), with 14% from other European countries (the Netherlands, Norway, Poland, and Switzerland).

The majority of the European executives we interviewed are males (81%) in the age range of 40 to 49 years. Seventy-six percent of the European executives have at least a university level of education.

General demographic data on the European derailment and success cases can be obtained from the background information question asked during the interviews. The majority of the derailment and success cases are male. Only 4% of the case studies are female. The Europeans in our case studies are educated. Only 6% of the derailment and 7% of the success cases have earned only a high school degree. Most of the success cases (N=93) and the derailment cases (N=76) are senior-level executives.

Data Collection

As in much previous CCL derailment research, these executives were asked to think of two managers they knew well (North Americans in the U.S. case, Europeans in the E.U.): (1) a manager who had made it to the top of his or her organization, and (2) a manager who had been seen as having senior management potential but who had not made it to the top and thus was not successful. The interviews (see Appendix A for interview questions) were conducted by one of five interviewers who were primarily located in Europe. The European interviews lasted from two to two-and-a-half hours, whereas the average North American interview lasted one hour. We suspect that the difference in interview length is a consequence of skill differences in the use of the English language, as well as the additional time required for interviewers to be certain about their interpretation of what was being communicated.

In addition to answering the interview questions, the senior executives completed a SYMLOG form designed to cross-validate our findings. SYMLOG® (Systematic Multiple-Level Observation of Groups) uses a 26-item questionnaire designed to measure values associated with leadership and teamwork. The form is located in Appendix B. (See Appendix C for quantitative results.)

Content Analysis

This is comparative research. As such, its intent is to identify differences between groups. We therefore chose to analyze the European and the North American data separately. We also chose not to use classification themes developed from the research conducted in the 1980s to allow for the emergence of differences over time.

Although we recognize that differences do exist among the value orientations of the different European cultures (Haire, Ghiselli, & Porter, 1966; Hall, 1981; Hofstede, 1984, 1991; Hofstede & Sami Kassem, 1976; Hoppe, 1990; Ronen & Kraut, 1977; Triandis & Bontempo, 1986; Triandis, McCusker, & Hui, 1990; Trompenaars, 1993), we did not separate the six European countries for purposes of these analyses. First, we did not have a large enough sample of interviewees to make the number significant in any one country. Second, many of the organizations in which we conducted interviews were located in more than one country. Given the fact that organizational culture may be as strong an influence in some situations as is national culture (Gopalan, 1991; Hofstede, 1990), it did not seem legitimate to split company data along national lines.

For both sets of data (European and North American), the open-ended responses were content-analyzed. Independently, four researchers analyzed the responses to the questions and noted themes throughout the interview material. The themes were then discussed and initial content themes were developed. The research team then specified which themes were present in each interviewee's data. The presence or absence of themes was discussed until agreement was reached and more refined content themes and definitions were developed. To test reliability, a different group of four researchers was given theme definitions and subsets of the data to classify. For each theme, the percentage of agreement between independent researchers was calculated. The percentages ranged from 84% to 100% for the European success factors and 91% to 98% for the European derailment factors. The reliability for the North American success factors ranged from 88% to 100%, while the North American derailment factors ranged from 93% to 100%.

Results and Discussion of Research on Executive Derailment in the 1990s

What Derails North American Managers?
Nine themes emerged from the North American derailment data (see Appendix D for complete listing and description of factors). Of these, only two derailment factors, the "Inability to develop or adapt" and "Poor working relationships," were mentioned by over 50% of the interviewees. Their descriptions are presented below.

Inability to develop or adapt. The most frequently cited reason for derailment among North American executives is the inability to develop or adapt. For several of these Americans (33%), the inability to change management style was a factor in their downfall. Others seemed stubborn or resistant to the point where they couldn't change.

> He couldn't change. He had a rigid and outdated management style. He was inflexible and people got tired of it.

Poor working relations. As in previous CCL studies of derailment, poor working relationships continues to top the list of reasons for derailment. These managers, in general, had difficulty with communicating, listening, trustworthiness, and being a team player. One derailed North American manager was described as follows:

> He left dead bodies everywhere. He would have people hanging out to dry if they wouldn't do what he wanted. He would push them to do what he wanted and then deny any involvement.

Comparison to Successful North American Executives
A total of 14 traits or skills were attributed to successful North American executives (see Appendix E). "Ability to develop or adapt," "Establishes

strong collaborative relationships," and "Intelligent" were emphasized by 50% or more of the interviewees.

Ability to develop or adapt. The most frequently mentioned success factor of North American managers (55%) is the ability to develop or adapt. Development for several of the managers was framed in terms of change that occurred as a result of direct feedback. For others, adaptability had to do with "maturing over time" and "growing" as the job or organization expanded. For example,

> She has grown as a person. She accepted challenges in her personal and professional life. She overcame enormous odds in her quest to success. As the organization grew she grew with it, she learned and took on more complexity.

Establishes strong collaborative relationships. Most senior executives noted the ability to work with others as important for success. The senior executives described leaders as enhancing good relationships by sending people cards on their birthdays, listening, supporting others' ideas, and making themselves available to help. They also described successful leaders as "team players." For example, one successful North American manager was described as:

> Very personable, easy to talk with (he made good eye contact, used open body language), very caring. He would seek input from people of all levels. He utilized the staff well. He made you feel as if you were truly a contributor by listening and getting feedback. He was the first to implement teams.

Intelligent. Of no surprise, senior executives attributed leaders' success to their "intelligence," "high IQ," or "brilliance." As one senior executive noted of a successful executive:

> He came to the attention of some senior managers early on for his curiosity and intelligence.

What Derails European Managers?

Among European executives, only two derailment flaws were mentioned by a majority of senior executives interviewed; a total of 10 derailment factors were identified overall (see Appendix F for a complete listing and description of factors). The two derailment factors, "Poor working relations" and the "Inability to develop or adapt," are described below.

Poor working relations. The most frequently mentioned derailment factor (64%) involves poor relationships. Interviewees often described managers with this "fatal" characteristic as insensitive, manipulative, critical, demanding, and not trustworthy. One derailed European manager was described as follows:

> He was always criticizing others, he felt free to do so without taking any responsibility for himself. . . . His relationships with subordinates were not sound; he could be over-friendly but not over-concerned. His behavior was arrogant. In fact he used other people for his ambition. When he hired people he looked for people like himself, mirror images. Always a mistake. He left the company two years ago and I think that he is still looking for a job.

Other European managers lacked a teamwork orientation. Interviewees described them as being solitary, a "lone wolf," not a team player, or simply unable to communicate effectively.

Authoritarian management style also is noted by senior executives in Europe in conjunction with poor working relationships. Some derailed European managers were characterized as having ruled by fear, as being dictatorial.

> People were quitting or requesting transfers. She expected complete loyalty, to the extreme. She was dictatorial, overly protective of the group and her own ideas which she forced onto the group. Once someone left, she barely said hello to them after that, and their accomplishments were forgotten. She tried to isolate the team almost completely from the other departments and the outside world, cutting all the links. That way her people couldn't learn about how other units functioned, how other managers behaved.

Inability to develop or adapt. Many of the interviewees cited examples of managers' inability to adapt, their inflexibility, and narcissism as reasons for derailment. "Absolutely egotistical" and "pig-headed" were commonly used descriptions of flaws that kept managers from changing or advancing. In many of the cases, the senior executives gave the managers feedback on areas for improvement. For whatever reasons, the derailed managers were unable to learn from feedback and apply the recommendations.

> I was coaching her. We had many sessions together where the problems were identified and we tried to come up with an action plan. Some problems she "owned," others she didn't. She really didn't change. She would change for a week or two, then return to base line. (European, 1994)

Resistance to cultural change or the inability to adapt to the habits and culture of the company was another common description of this flaw. For some of these managers, company culture changed with mergers. Other managers had difficulty adjusting to another country's culture. One senior executive from an organization in Europe said of a derailed manager:

> He is beyond 50 and is not flexible; is unwilling to adapt himself to new organizations and people's needs.

Comparison to Successful European Executives

Four factors appeared for the majority of managers who made it to the top. The factors include the "Ability to develop or adapt," "Consistent exceptional performance," "Establishes strong collaborative relationships," and "Business and technical expertise." Explanations and examples of these factors are provided below. A total of 18 success factors were mentioned by the senior executives interviewed (see Appendix G).

Ability to develop or adapt. Managers' willingness to develop or adapt is the success factor most often cited by the senior executives (cited in 67% of the success cases). The type of learning spanned several areas such as learning the business, learning from mistakes, learning from direct feedback, and learning that specifically enhances self-development. For example, one European senior executive described a success case as follows:

> He was first assigned to one of our subsidiaries to learn purchasing and manufacturing, and then afterwards became the general manager for several countries, all subsidiaries. . . . Those last two years were very fruitful in terms of learning for our man, who now really understands the whole business. . . . He was a good student, more than willing to listen and learn from bosses and experience.

Another European senior executive, reflecting on the climate of rapid change, said:

> Our industry was characterized by nationalization and privatization and periods of recession which were rapid and unpredictable. We were affected by global disorder and the fragile nature of the world economy. America and Japan exercised control. There was an emphasis on changing culture and the attitudes of people. One needed to understand different cultures, especially European and Japanese: "Think globally, act locally." The company was over-structured and top-heavy with a "squelchy" middle management. Those who survived were efficient, flexible, and versatile.

Consistent exceptional performance. It is no surprise that our research confirmed the importance of obtaining results in a successful career. Early on, "the ability to perform the job" and be "results oriented" were often factors that initially caught the eye of upper management (cited in 57% of the cases). For most of these managers, exceptional performance remained a factor throughout their careers.

> He excelled at each job he did. From the company point of view, he excelled in delivering results.

Establishes strong collaborative relationships. The ability to work with others appears to be an important characteristic for success. Interviewees mentioned good relationships with bosses, peers, and subordinates as common factors for success in 57% of the cases.

> [He has] a capacity to establish a very strong relationship with people. He is able to embody the company's mission with his behavior. He always takes the time to shake hands with subordinates and make them feel important. He genuinely cares for people.

Business and technical expertise. Fifty-two percent of the senior executives attributed managers' early success to their business or technical expertise. This factor was often mentioned by senior executives as a quality that first caught the eye of important managers in their organizations.

Summary

With respect to executives in the 1990s, a total of 10 flaws that can lead executives to derailment were identified (see Table 1). The top two derailment factors for North Americans and Europeans are "Poor working relations" and the "Inability to develop or adapt."

Table 1
Derailment Factors Most Frequently Mentioned
by Senior Executives in the 1990s

Derailment Factors	Percentage of Cases	
	Europeans	*North Americans*
Poor working relations	64	50
Inability to develop or adapt	62	60
Inability to build and lead a team	24	40
Not prepared for promotion	18	10
Too ambitious	18	15
Poor performance	16	30
Authoritarian	16	30
Too narrow functional orientation	13	20
Conflict with upper management	13	10
Organizational isolation	13	0

As we stated at the beginning of the report, senior executives were asked to describe successful executives as well as derailed ones as a way to contrast the two groups. A comparison of the most frequently mentioned characteristics for successful leadership in the 1990s to the most frequently cited characteristics of the derailed reveals a mirroring effect (summarized in Table 2).

Not surprisingly, the characteristics are opposites. At least one factor, however—"Ambition"—appears to be a strength which, in excess, can lead to derailment. This would suggest that executives should be cautious not to overuse their strengths.

Focusing on fatal flaws often disguises the fact that most of these executives had achieved high-level positions prior to their derailment. For many of them, the inability to learn and develop probably sealed their fate.

Table 2
Success Factors Compared to Derailment Factors in the 1990s

Characteristics of Successful Leaders	*Characteristics of Derailed Leaders*
Ability to develop or adapt	Inability to develop or adapt
Establishes strong collaborative relations	Poor working relations
Ability to build and lead a team	Inability to build and lead a team
Non-authoritarian	Authoritarian
Consistent exceptional performance	Poor performance
Ambitious	Too ambitious

Possessing any single fatal flaw or success characteristic is not enough to predict the outcome of one's career. A combination of these factors contributes to managers' eventual outcome, but as these data suggest, complete absence of the success factors (listed in Table 2) can lead to derailment.

North American and European Derailment: A Few Differences

The derailment themes present in the European interviews are, for the most part, consistent with those in the North American interviews. Yet there are differences worth noting.

One aspect of the European interviews that departed from the North American interviews has to do with salience of the background question asked in all interviews in both studies. At the start of each interview, we asked the senior executives to give us some background information on both the successful and derailed managers they had prepared to talk with us about. Typically, executives in the U.S. cited employment history in response to this question (for example, whether the manager had spent his or her entire career with the company or had worked elsewhere, original functional specialty, job history). In the interviews we conducted in Europe, however, many executives went beyond facts about career to include in their background sketch some mention of the perceived social class of the individual, noting things like "upper class origin," "high middle class," or "suspect he was from a poor family." Also, the Europeans were more likely to mention the prestige level of the university the manager attended, for example "very prestigious French university" or "university of only moderate prestige."[1] This difference probably reflects a greater inclination on the part of Europeans to recognize ascribed bases of status than is true among North Americans, who tend to focus more on status that is achieved. Again, this may be a cultural value difference among European countries, with some being more likely than others to refer to ascribed bases of status such as social class.

Although this aspect of the European interviews did differ from the North American, when interview questions turned to actual reasons for success or derailment, these background characteristics were not mentioned directly. Thus, they are not included in our main discussion of derailment in this paper.

Another difference between the European and North American interviews has to do with the nature of the derailment factor and problems with interpersonal relationships. Although most of the descriptors used by European and North American senior executives are the same, the people we interviewed in Europe highlighted one aspect, authoritarianism, more than the North American interviewees did. The only time authoritarian style was mentioned in a U.S. derailment interview, it was set in the context of the manager's inability to adapt to change in the organizational culture. This subtle difference may indicate that the organizational culture change toward more participative leadership, that has characterized organizations in the U.S. over the past five to ten years, may just be of relevance in European organizations. European senior executives see an authoritarian style as a factor in derailment. They did not talk about an organizational shift away from this management style as a factor in the derailment of these managers. This difference may also relate to a cultural difference on the power distance dimension described by Hofstede (1984). *Power distance* refers to the extent to which people accept and expect that power is distributed unequally. Although the different countries that comprise our sample do have different locations on the power distance dimension, it may be that our interviews are picking up a cultural difference that exists in only two or three countries.

Finally, one derailment factor, "Organizational isolation," was evident only in the European interviews. Managers who possess this flaw were described as "isolated" or as people who placed boundaries around their unit, department, or function.

Quantitative Support: SYMLOG® Results

Every methodology has its limitations. Qualitative or interview-based research (such as the research described here) is a useful means of collecting rich data on salient aspects of leadership effectiveness within a culture. Although qualitative data can have a richness lacking in quantitative measurement techniques, it can lack the measurement precision (or appearance of precision) found in instruments.

Quantitative methods, in the form of reliable and valid instruments or questionnaires, allow one to measure, with some precision, dimensions that have been shown to be related to important constructs like effective leadership. Yet many of these tools are based on research and theory originally developed in one culture (often the U.S.) and subsequently tested in others. Even when these subsequent tests show the given dimensions to be significantly related to effective leadership in other cultures, one cannot know, using these tools alone, what vital elements may be missing.

Since these issues are particularly relevant in a cross-cultural study, we incorporated into our design a means of comparing results using two methods. At the conclusion of each face-to-face interview on success and derailment, we asked the interviewee to complete a SYMLOG® form on the success case they had described, as well as on the case of a derailed executive.

We chose SYMLOG for two reasons. First, it has been used in a wide variety of contexts and situations throughout the world. The instrument has proven reliable and valid for use by managers in the U.S. and in many countries in Europe (see Van Velsor & Leslie, 1991, pp. 255-274). Secondly, it measures individual and organizational values for teamwork and provides a measure of "most effective profile" for leaders of task-oriented work groups (see Appendix C for fuller description of instrument). Since we know that SYMLOG is a reliable measure of the values related to leadership, scores on its dimensions should differentiate those described as successful from those described as derailed in our interviews. In addition, its profiles of successful and derailed managers should correspond to the factors identified in our interviews as characteristic of these two groups.

Our analysis of the SYMLOG data collected during these interviews provides clear support for the contrast between the characteristics of successful and derailed managers (see Figures 1 and 2 in Appendix C). SYMLOG clearly differentiates the successful (circle labeled SUL) from the derailed (circle labeled DRD) for both North American and European executives. The location of the successful managers (SUL circle) in the diagrams suggests that both successful Europeans and North Americans are close to the "most effective profile" (MEP) and perceived by their senior executives to place a moderate emphasis on values associated with dominance, acceptance of authority, and being friendly. In other words, the successful executives are likely to behave in an assertive, analytical, task-oriented, problem-solving, egalitarian, cooperative manner while being unconcerned with status differences and disagreement.

There is some similarity, too, between North American and European derailed executives (DRD circles in the diagrams). In general, these executives are seen by those at the top of their organizations as unfriendly and negativistic.

A few subtle differences do occur, however, between the derailed Europeans and the North Americans. The derailed Europeans are located below the U.S. derailed executives on the SYMLOG dimension that reflects the acceptance of the established authority around tasks. In other words, the derailed European may be perceived as isolated, in opposition to upper management, and in disagreement with others' attempts to preserve solidarity, equality, and common rewards for the good of the group as a whole. There is also a slight difference in the size of the groups' circles. Although this difference is probably insignificant, the derailed European group's circle is a little larger than the North American derailed group's circle.

Overall SYMLOG results emphasize the perceptions of the derailed Europeans as domineering and powerful (reflected in the "Authoritarian" theme in our interview data), having excessive dependence upon self (reflected in the "Organizational isolation" theme in our interviews), in opposition to authority (reflected in the "Conflict with upper management" theme in the interview data), and unfriendly (reflected in the interview themes "Poor working relations" and "Inability to build and lead a team"). Two cases from the interview data exemplify the unfriendly, oppositional (SYMLOG) values of a derailer profile.

> He was reluctant to communicate with his hierarchical boss. He was communicating with his boss's boss. He had an enormous ego, therefore he failed to recognize a superior in the most general terms! He had peculiarities, he exercised in his office and walked around in bare feet. He perceived that everything is allowed for him. He thought of himself as a super manager.

> He often used his "big mouth" to make rude statements about the company's policies. He could not cooperate in broad matters. Became negative, wanted to be a "lone wolf."

Comparison of CCL Derailment Themes Over Time

Enduring Derailment Themes

Comparing CCL's derailment factors from research in the 1980s, 1990s, and across cultures reveals four dominant derailment themes (see Table 3). They are classified as (1) Problems with Interpersonal Relationships, (2) Failure to Meet Business Objectives, (3) Inability to Build and Lead a Team, and (4) Inability to Change or Adapt During a Transition.[2]

Problems with Interpersonal Relationships. Problems with Interpersonal Relationships is the theme that, more than any other, reveals the negative aspects of character that derail managers. This category describes the personality characteristics seen as getting in the way of effective leadership. In this research, managers who are seen as having problems with interpersonal relationships are described by others as insensitive, manipulative, critical, demanding, authoritarian, self-isolating, or aloof.

Across studies and over time, the characteristics grouped together here are some of the most frequently mentioned factors in derailment. Insensitivity to others and being perceived as cold, aloof, and arrogant were hallmarks of derailment in the earliest CCL derailment research (McCall & Lombardo, 1983). As can be seen in Table 3, poor relationships was a factor in the derailment of women, as well as in factor analyses of questionnaire data. In the recent derailment research, Problems with Interpersonal Relationships was mentioned in two-thirds of the cases in Europe, while more than one-third of recently derailed North American managers were seen as having poor working relationships.[3]

It should be noted that the interpersonal relationships theme in CCL's derailment research relates to the relationship or consideration dimension of the well-known task/relationship model of leadership behavior (Blake & Mouton, 1985; Fleishman, 1953; Hersey & Blanchard; 1988; Likert, 1961; Stogdill & Coons, 1957). That is, the derailment theme executives describe as Problems with Interpersonal Relationships appears to be a deficit in the area of relationship behavior. People who are successful early in their careers appear to be proficient in task-based leadership but are presented with a challenge when job demands begin to require a balance with a more relationship-oriented style (see also Shipper & Dillard, 1994).

In the 1990s, as before, managers who derailed in both Europe and the U.S. often were described as insensitive and manipulative.

Table 3
Four Enduring Derailment Themes in CCL's Derailment Research

McCall & Lombardo (1983)	Morrison et al. (1987)	Lombardo & McCauley (1988)	U.S.A. (1993-94)	Europe (1993-94)	
Insensitive to others	Poor relationships	Problems with interpersonal relationships	Poor working relations	Poor working relations	*Problems with Interpersonal Relationships*
Cold, aloof, arrogant					
		Isolates self		Organizational isolation	
			Authoritarian	Authoritarian	
Overly ambitious	Too ambitious			Too ambitious	
Betrayal of trust		Lack of follow-through	Too ambitious	Too ambitious	*Failure to Meet Business Objectives*
Poor performance	Performance problems		Poor performance	Poor performance	
Failing to staff effectively	Can't manage subordinates	Difficulty molding a staff	Inability to build and lead a team	Inability to build and lead a team	*Inability to Build and Lead a Team*
Unable to adapt to a boss with a different style	Unable to adapt to a boss or culture		Unable to develop or adapt	Unable to develop or adapt	*Inability to Change or Adapt During a Transition*
		Strategic differences with management	Conflict with upper management	Conflict with upper management	
Unable to think strategically	Not strategic	Difficulty making strategic transitions			

Table 3a
An Emergent and a Disappearing Theme in CCL's Derailment Research

McCall & Lombardo (1983)	Morrison et al. (1987)	Lombardo & McCauley (1988)	U.S.A. (1993-94)	Europe (1993-94)
An Emergent Theme				
			Not prepared for promotion	Not prepared for promotion
	Too narrow business experience		Narrow functional orientation	Narrow functional orientation
. . . .				
A Disappearing Theme				
Overdependent on advocate or mentor	Overdependence			
. . . .				

He was a bad people manager . . . a manipulator of people. He started creating a poor climate in the office, making the work life not productive. After several warnings, he was fired. (European, 1993)

He is a great strategic thinker and he has high ethical standards, but he lashes out at people, he can't build trusting relationships. He is very smart, but he achieves superiority through demeaning others. He is abusive, he hits people with intellectual lightning. He instinctively goes after people. Many people have tried to work on this flaw because he has such extraordinary skills, but it seems hopeless. (North American, 1994)

Being overly critical and using others to further one's own ambitions are aspects of poor interpersonal relations that have been noted as factors throughout CCL's derailment research, and are present still in the recent data.

Finally, Problems with Interpersonal Relationships also includes managers who are described as being solitary or unwilling to communicate. For example:

> He was not interested in communicating with his team, co-workers or peers; not committed to sharing and transferring experience, information, knowledge, or process. He tended to be a block in the flow of information, a bottleneck within the company. (European, 1993)

And of another derailed executive, we heard:

> He was too individualistic. He was not a team worker, and unable to work with others. A one-man show. He did not accept belonging to a big company. (European, 1993)

Although Problems with Interpersonal Relationships is one derailment factor that endures over time and across the cultures considered here, this does not mean that all managers who have problems with interpersonal relationships will derail, or that problems with interpersonal relationships (or any other single derailment factor) will lead to derailment in all organizations. In the questionnaire-based study conducted by Lombardo and McCauley (1988), problems with interpersonal relationships was correlated with the likelihood of derailment in some organizations but not in others. This factor appears to be one that has much to do with the organizational culture. It also may be the case that even if a manager derails for a combination of reasons, problems with interpersonal relationships is one of the most obvious explanations for derailment, after the fact.

Failure to Meet Business Objectives. In every CCL derailment study, a track record of performance has been a typical reason given for derailed managers' early successes. Early in their careers, when the job required technical skills or making and implementing decisions on one's own in a relatively stable system, the derailed managers were seen as able to meet business objectives. But as conditions changed, requiring new skills and ways of working with others, productivity problems began to arise for the derailers.

> He had very disappointing business results. The marketplace competition was tight and at that time there were poor quality products to sell, but there was a great pressure to produce profits. There were wrong strategic decisions made. In general, corporate headquarters was very upset. His very senior level position was a make or break position but he could not produce results. He left the company and is now general manager of another business. (North American, 1994)

Failure to meet performance expectations has been identified as a source of derailment throughout CCL's program of research. In the early CCL derailment research (Lombardo & McCauley, 1988; McCall & Lombardo, 1983), not meeting business objectives was attributed to a lack of follow-through on promises or to being overly ambitious. Often, the failure to deliver results was seen as a betrayal of trust or unjustified self-promotion.

The case of self-promotion without the deliverables to support it was cited by many European senior executives in recent interviews about derailment. One interviewee offered this account:

> He was very ambitious and spent a lot of time demonstrating it by telling others "I want to replace Mr. X or Y: I deserve it. I'm in a position to replace him." But there was no demonstration of competence to accompany this ambition. Over time, he demonstrated that he was less competent for the job he had. . . . He is not trusted by *internal* customers in the field. They didn't see him as credible, knowledgeable enough to be competent.

Inability to Build and Lead a Team. Typically, a manager who derails does so for several closely related reasons. For some, the inability to build and lead a team may have led to the failure to meet business objectives. The inability to build and lead a team also may be related to some of the more personality or relationship-oriented factors described in the earlier section.

The Inability to Build and Lead a Team was an important derailment factor mentioned in one out of four of the European interviews and in one out of five of the North American cases. One European executive described a manager who derailed as follows:

> When he reached a position where he had to deal with significant numbers of people at different levels, he could not do it. He was very isolated, did not create a team, was over-confident, tough and individualistic. (European, 1993)

Kovach (1986), as well as McCall and Lombardo (1983), point out that the traits, such as assertiveness and initiative, that put a manager on the fast track early on tend to be the same traits that get in the way as individuals face the transition to a teamwork approach often required at the executive level. Barbara Kovach's (1986) work on derailment emphasizes the shifts in expectations that go with changes in career phase and organizational level from early career/functional orientation to later career/organizational overview. Early in their careers, managers are rewarded for independence and decisiveness within the context of narrowly defined areas of influence (e.g., functions or departments). Later, managers are expected to work effectively within the larger context of the total organization and its external environment and to recognize and influence the interdependence that characterizes such systems.

Kaplan, Drath, and Kofodimos (1991) echo this theme in their work, based on intense interview studies with North American senior executives. Expansive executives, according to Kaplan, are those executives who depend on achievement and success as a means of obtaining and reinforcing a sense of self-worth. He contrasts these with the relational type, who seek communion or connectedness in order to build self-worth. The ability to use a more relational orientation, to strike a balance between "mastery over" and "connection to" is critical to success at higher levels.

In addition to increased salience of a team orientation as one moves up, for many senior executives the ability to build and lead a team also is critical because it is related to a shift in leadership style they see as important. One North American senior executive told us:

> Today, the leadership skills required are different, even from five years ago. The expectations of people around style have changed greatly. A manager can no longer rely on position power to get the job done. People want to see their leaders, hear them talk from their hearts, roll their sleeves up and spontaneously and genuinely build that trust. Followership is critical, especially in downsizing organizations. People don't want to see you only when there is a downsizing announcement to be made. People want to know what's in it for them and if the person leading them knows and cares about them enough. Today, if you're going to spill your blood for the organization, it will be because of personal loyalty to your team, not to some abstract organization.

One North American executive described a derailed manager's early success as follows:

> . . . at that time, these things (e.g., building a team) were not important. But the culture has changed. It used to be hard-nosed and authoritarian. In that context a manager could make decisions on his own, implement those, and be seen as successful. He has not been able to make this transition.

Inability to Change or Adapt During a Transition. Another theme in CCL's derailment research over time has to do with a manager's ability to adapt to the change required during a transition. When examined across studies, the theme has several elements, including failure to adapt to a new boss with a different style; overdependence on a single skill and/or failure to acquire new skills; and an inability to adapt to the demands of a new job, a new culture, or changes in the market (see Table 3).

Yet despite its persistence over time, this is a theme that appears to have evolved in its meaning and salience to senior executives. When adaptability was mentioned in the early McCall and Lombardo interviews (1983), it was chiefly in connection with adapting to a new boss with a different style. Overdependence on a boss or mentor was a key derailment factor and the inability to be open to new ways of working required by a different boss helped get many managers off the track. In the later work by Lombardo and McCauley (1988), overdependence on a single mentor or on a narrow set of skills was a factor that appeared in their analyses of questionnaire data, although it was not one of the factors with a strong relationship to derailment. However, inability to adapt was one of the critical factors in the derailment of women managers, perhaps because women (or anyone seen as different by the dominant culture) may experience more pressure to change or adapt to that culture.

Today, both in Europe and the United States, senior executives appear to be putting a great deal more emphasis on the importance of being able to change or develop as a result of a transition (in job, culture, or organization), as well as on the importance of adapting one's thinking to changes in the market than they once did. In addition to the inability to develop in relation to a job transition or promotion, many of the European and North American senior executives we interviewed cited examples of managers' inability to adapt to changes in the organizational culture, the environment, or the market as reasons for their derailment.

In recent interviews, this inflexibility often is described as an inability to change one's management style toward a more participative or team-based approach. Many of the managers who were seen as unable to adapt to change also were caught in a changing organizational culture and were seen as unable to build and lead a team, as described in the previous section.

While resistance to change in the organizational culture was a common flaw of both the North Americans and Europeans, managers in Europe also are likely to derail because of difficulty adjusting to another country's culture. The inability to adjust to a different culture did not appear to be a factor in the derailment of U.S. managers. This is not to say that North American managers do not have difficulty in this area but that the senior executives we interviewed did not call it out as an important aspect of derailment, possibly because expatriating and having to relocate to another country was not part of their career requirements.

In many of the cases, the senior executives described repeated efforts to give the managers feedback on areas for improvement. For whatever reason, the derailed managers were unable or unwilling to learn from or apply the feedback.

A combination of problems with interpersonal relationships and aspects of inability to adapt can manifest as a conflict with higher management. The majority of managers described as having conflict with senior management did not agree with their boss(es) and were generally critical. For example, one European senior executive remarked:

> He showed impatience, too much impatience, and bumped up against his boss regarding business strategy: "*I* know what to do and I don't think that you know as well as I do." So this guy alienated his boss— the person who could have opened the path to the senior job. He represents the classic case of getting rejected/blocked by the system. If one doesn't play the game, it doesn't work.

When the inability to develop or adapt was related to a change in the nature or scope of one's job, a derailed manager's plight was often attributed to a lack of depth or "too narrow a functional orientation" as they were moved up the organizational ladder. When they were given the responsibility for much broader cross-functional areas of the organization, never having had the opportunity to stretch their views in more limited ways, they derailed. Although senior managers in the earliest research did not directly attribute derailment to having had a narrow functional orientation, McCall and Lombardo's (1983) comparison of the career histories of successful and derailed managers showed that derailers were far more likely to have had the same set of experiences over and over, and that managers who continued to be seen as successful had been in a wide variety of jobs.

Comparison to Enduring Success Themes

A review of CCL's derailment research compares eight success themes that appear to have endured over time and across cultures (see Table 4). The themes are classified as (1) Ambitious, (2) Establishes Strong Relationships, (3) Consistently High Performance, (4) Team-building and Leadership Skills,

(5) Intelligence, (6) Willingness to Take Risks, (7) Able to Adapt, and
(8) Problem-solver.

Ambitious. Not surprisingly, successful leaders in our research, McCall
and Lombardo's (1983), and Morrison et al.'s (1987) research possess the
desire to succeed. In fact, 29% of the Europeans and 15% of the North
Americans in our study were labeled ambitious by senior executives. Ambitious leaders were most commonly described as driven and determined to
make it to the top of their organizations. One interviewee noted:

> He's the only person I ever met who told me right when we met that he
> wanted to become president and he said he wanted to do it in 15 years.
> He missed it by maybe 6 months but he's there! (European, 1994)

For many of the European and North American managers, ambition was
an asset that didn't interfere with their interpersonal relationships. One
executive offered this insight:

> He has a strong personal ambition but does not let it get in the way of
> the team, he makes decisions that are best for the company. (North
> American, 1994)

The ambition that drives managers to the top can have serious consequences on personal and family life. McCall and Lombardo (1983) were
among the first to note that executives make many sacrifices along the road to
the top. Morrison et al. (1987) also noted women's desire to succeed often
forced them to "choose their job before family." For the women, being
geographically mobile also seemed to be an indication of their dedication to
their careers. Embedded within the background information we often found
examples of European managers who were moved from country to country as
a result of their jobs. Although we did not use this background information to
determine whether or not they were ambitious, it does speak to some of the
sacrifices they must have made to make it to the top.

Establishes Strong Relationships. Throughout CCL's derailment
research, the ability to establish strong relationships has been critical to
managers' success. In the 1980s, managers were seen by others as getting
along with all kinds of people, outgoing, liked, charming, or easy to be with
(McCall & Lombardo, 1983; Morrison et al., 1987). Today, senior executives
use additional descriptors such as honest, trustworthy, straightforward, or

Table 4
Eight Enduring Success Themes in CCL's Derailment Research

McCall & Lombardo (1983)	Morrison et al. (1987)	U.S.A. (1993-94)	Europe (1993-94)	
Ambitious	Desire to succeed	Ambitious	Ambitious	*Ambitious*
Made many sacrifices				
Got along with all kinds of people	Easy to be with	Establishes strong collaborative relationships	Establishes strong collaborative relationships	*Establishes Strong Relationships*
Outgoing, liked, charming		Non-authoritarian	Non-authoritarian	
		Integrity	Integrity	
Outstanding track record	Good track record	Consistent exceptional performance	Consistent exceptional performance	*Consistently High Performance*
Excellent at motivating or directing subordinates	Can manage subordinates	Able to build and lead a team	Able to build and lead a team	*Team-building & Leadership Skills*
Incredibly bright	Smart	Intelligent	Intelligent	*Intelligence*
Took career risks	Took career risks	Willingness to take risks	Willingness to take risks	*Willingness to Take Risks*

(continued)

Table 4 (continued)
Eight Enduring Success Themes in CCL's Derailment Research

McCall & Lombardo (1983)	Morrison et al. (1987)	U.S.A. (1993-94)	Europe (1993-94)	
Maintained composure under stress	Able to adapt to environment	Ability to develop and adapt	Ability to develop and adapt	*Able to Adapt*
Handled mistakes with poise and grace				
. . . .				
Focused on problems and solved them		Problem-solver and entrepreneurial	Problem-solver and entrepreneurial	*Problem-solver*
. . . .				

ethical to describe successful managers whose integrity has helped them to establish good working relations. An executive offered this example:

> He was very personable, easy to talk with. He was also very credible. This is because he would get the facts before he said anything. He would follow through on things. He was very caring, straightforward, a most successful manager. (North American, 1994)

For the managers in our research, integrity seemed to typify a consistency and predictability others come to expect.

The ability to work with others was cited as a success factor by 64% of the European and 50% of the North American senior executives. Managers who established strong relationships with bosses, peers, and subordinates did so by listening, making themselves available, and sharing responsibility. One European executive remarked of another:

> He had a great belief that working democratically would benefit all workers. He was honest, collaborative, and open to new ideas. He was a great supporter of people and people's ideas. He made himself acces-

sible to everyone in the company. He was extremely ethical and dependable.

Many of the successful North American and European managers, who were seen as open to others' ideas and cultures, were also described as non-authoritarian leaders. These managers enhanced working relationships through empowering others to share ideas and then supporting them, and seeking feedback from people at all organizational levels. In addition, many of the successful leaders in the 1990s established good working relations as a result of their teamwork orientation.

> He pitches in, he is a team player. He spends more time with people at work than family because he thinks that it is important that everyone gets along and enjoys work. He tries to create an environment that is pleasant and enjoyable. His philosophy is to treat others as he wants to be treated with promotions. He thinks of "is this how I want to be treated?" He respects people regardless of differences. (North American, 1994)

Models of effective leadership styles have for a long time included behaviors that were human relations-oriented as well as task-oriented (Blake & Mouton, 1985; Ekvall & Arvonen, 1994; Fiedler, 1967, 1971; Fleishman, 1953; Hersey & Blanchard, 1988; Likert, 1961; Stogdill & Coons, 1957). Our research findings support both of these dimensions, as the first two enduring success themes—Establishes Strong Relationships and Consistently High Performance—highlight.

Consistently High Performance. Outstanding track records of performance have clearly been hallmarks of successful executives in this series of research (McCall & Lombardo, 1983; Morrison et al., 1987). Early in the careers of North American and European managers, the ability to get the job done and obtain desired results often got them noticed by upper management. One senior executive offered this example of a successful leader:

> The results of her work made her noticed. She made money [for the company] by being analytical and systematic in obtaining results. For example, she created a net retention system that allowed the company to assess their profit. (European, 1993)

And, as these managers moved into more complex, cross-functional positions, their performance remained consistently high. For instance, one senior executive reported:

> He has had a consistent performance in our organization. He has a steady climb, he has assumed more responsibility, more commitment, loyalty, and has achieved organization credibility. I think that his consistent record of achievement has been the single thing that contributed most to his success to the top. (North American, 1994)

It is of no surprise that stability in performance has remained a success factor over time and across cultures. The most striking feature about this theme in the 1990s concerns the turbulent environments in which these managers have been able to maintain excellent performances.

Team-building and Leadership Skills. The ability to lead others has remained a characteristic of successful executives over time and across cultures. These managers have been skilled at communicating with team members, motivating, delegating, and selecting team members who can work together and produce results. Spoken by an interviewee:

> He sets clear goals and lets others know what is expected of them. He is very respected by others. He knows how to motivate others to reach his goals. He "lets them grow their own garden." (North American, 1994)

Another executive noted:

> He built a team around him who could work together and produce results. His success depended on that. He hired people who could not only do the job but who could work together. (European, 1993)

The ability to build and lead a team was an important success factor in 40% of the North American and 24% of the European success cases.

Intelligence. McCall and Lombardo (1983) were the first CCL derailment researchers to highlight managers' intelligence in conjunction with their successes. In our research, 50% of the North American and 43% of the European senior executives point out this characteristic as one that put managers on the upward track early in their careers. One North American senior executive noted:

He first came to the attention of some senior managers for his curiosity and intelligence.

In the study of leadership, intelligence has been recognized as an important personal trait in a cross-section of studies (Cornwell, 1983; Lord, DeVader, & Alliger, 1986; Mann, 1959; Stogdill, 1948) as well as in longitudinal ones (Ball, 1983; Howard & Bray, 1988). According to Bass and Stogdill (1990), general intelligence influences one's ability to communicate, work with numbers, spatial orientation, and abstraction. In the following example, we can see support for how one manager's intellect may have influenced other characteristics noted in his success:

> His intellect first caught the eye of upper management and held it over the years. He had a vast knowledge of the field. He was a *quick study*. Others marvel and awe at his knowledge—he knows everything and can express it! He could conceptualize large systems easily. He also has the ability to articulate complex ideas clearly. (North American, 1994)

McCall and Lombardo (1983) were also the first in this line of CCL derailment researchers to attribute managers' failure to lack of competence in high-level tasks. This research points out that as managers reach higher level positions in organizations, not only are good interpersonal skills necessary but cognitive competence to effectively deal with complex problems is required.

Willingness to Take Risks. Successful leaders in our study, McCall and Lombardo's (1983), and Morrison et al.'s (1987) research are seen by senior executives as willing to take risks in the face of failure. A North American senior executive noted:

> She accepted the challenges of the middle level and moved up into the big leagues. It took a lot of guts on her part.

In our research, the risks primarily centered on taking on new jobs or tasks, but for some of the Europeans, risk also included moving themselves and their families to other countries. It is not uncommon for leaders to take calculated risks or use their intuition to make decisions with limited information. These executives, however, faced a higher level of risk failure because they were taking on new jobs *and* moving their families to countries foreign to their own. We can get a feel for one European manager's journey from a senior executive's background description.

When I first met him he was being looked at for a European marketing position in the U.K. The big test was to leave Italy—Italians don't like to leave Italy. He and his wife and their son moved to London. He put his son straight into an English school although he did not speak a word of English. He [executive] integrated well . . . came to love the U.K. Then he was selected to go to Paris to set up a regional office for Southern Europe. When he left the U.K. he actually burst in tears. It was a major organizational change in Paris. He moved an entire management team from one company in the space of 48 hours. It was a major test for a bigger leadership role and he came through it strongly! . . . Later he was given responsibility for all of Europe. And then he was promoted to the U.S.A. He was uneasy in that role but he drew what he needed to draw from the North American experience. A year later, after arriving in the U.S.A., an organizational change brought him back to run Europe and the Middle East.

Able to Adapt. Today, senior executives seem to be placing more value on the ability to adapt and develop than ever before. Among the North Americans and the Europeans, this success factor was cited in two-thirds of the success cases. When McCall and Lombardo (1983) first interviewed senior executives, the ability to adapt was reflected in managers' ability to maintain composure under stress and their handling of mistakes with poise and grace. Although McCall and Lombardo found that successful executives made few mistakes, when they did, they forewarned others so they wouldn't be blindsided by it and then began analyzing and fixing the error. Once they had handled the situation, they did not wallow in their mistake but moved on, suggesting an openness to learning.

In our study, the ability to adapt and develop was most often referenced in terms of managers' learning. Interviewees spoke of successful managers learning the business, learning from mistakes, learning from direct feedback, and learning for the purpose of enhancing self-development.

He was very aware of his strengths and limitations, he got help during a transition. He sought advice from HR. We set up a special program to get him in-depth assessment. People see him as open to feedback and change, and he actively works on these. He is very reflective of mistakes, he wants to learn from them. He is always talking about improving the system so this won't happen again. (North American, 1994)

For others, adapting and developing was described as "having matured." Interviewees referred to them as becoming "more relaxed," "more
flexible," "self-controlling," and "more self-assured" over time.

> He is very much more on the middle ground in behavior and in profes-
> sional outlook. He looks for the middle ground, he no longer takes the
> extremes. He has matured. And his politics have changed somewhat as
> well (e.g., at a conference he'd suddenly say, "Let's take half a day off
> and have a look at the city," when the agenda had been completely
> prepared for a two-day meeting). (European, 1993)

The persistence of this theme over time and across cultures, and the
magnitude to which it was emphasized as important for success today, sup-
ports Ekvall and Arvonen's (1994) research on leadership styles and effectiveness. The authors studied leadership styles in a range of countries, industries, and organizational levels. They found unequivocal evidence for a three-
factor model of style which incorporates task-oriented and people-oriented
factors, and a change-oriented factor. The emergence of the newer third
factor, change and development, they presume to be a consequence of more
turbulent environments. Leaders who were reported by subordinates to be
high on the change and development dimension were promoters of change
and growth, creative in their attitude, risk-takers, and visionaries. Ekvall and
Arvonen found leaders today to be more spread along this dimension,
whereas leaders in earlier decades may not have been because change was not
important during more stable times.

Problem-solver. Forty-five percent of the Europeans and 20% of the
North Americans referenced managers' ability to solve problems as a characteristic of the successful. Among the Europeans, it was not uncommon to find
this particular factor mentioned as a characteristic that contributed to managers being recognized early in their careers by senior management. As one
European senior executive noted:

> His disciplined thinking and problem solving; tenacity in problem
> solving [first caught the eye of important managers in the company].

Like McCall and Lombardo (1983), successful executives in the 1990s
focused on understanding "the problem" and were persistent in solving it.
What wasn't captured in the 1980s was the creativity and innovation being
used in the 1990s to implement new procedures.

Differences Over Time

Although four derailment themes and eight success themes have remained consistent over time, their interpretations seem to be shifting. These
shifts reflect the changing and ever more complex demands on managers in
more highly matrixed and often downsized organizations operating in global
markets.

Several differences stand out in comparing earlier U.S. studies to recent
derailment interviews. First, in the view of senior managers, the ability to
adapt and develop in the face of change or transition is more important now
than ever before. It appears to be a factor in two-thirds of all derailments both
in Europe and in the United States. In fact, one issue mentioned in previous
research but not found in recent interviews—strategic differences with
management—is likely now to be seen as part of a larger failure on the part of
the manager to adapt to a change in the market or the organizational culture.

In a sense, our study is as much a study of how senior executives
understand the competencies managers need as it is a study of what actually
derails managers. As the organizational environment has grown more uncer-
tain and the marketplace more global, senior executives appear to be using
different language to describe what is needed for success and what is involved in derailment. Rather than pointing to deficits in specific skills,
executives are recognizing that their most important need is to have managers
who can deal with change and complexity.

Our research confirms the results reported by Ekvall and Arvonen
(1994). Using large samples of managers from different countries, industries,
functions, and levels, these researchers found unequivocal support for a three-
factor model of leadership effectiveness, incorporating the well-known task-
and relationship-oriented behaviors and adding a third factor related to
change orientation.

A second difference over time also has to do, we suspect, with the
changing organizational context. Overdependence on a boss or mentor, an
important derailment factor in early studies, was not mentioned in the recent
interviews. It may be that, given the downsizing and turbulent environments
in organizations today, overdependence on a single boss or mentor has
become anachronistic. Of course, overdependence on a single skill, also
found in earlier studies, is very much a part of the ability to adapt and develop
in the face of change.

Interestingly, too, having a mentor play a strong role in managers'
career success was not found to be a success factor for North Americans in
the 1990s but it was for successful Europeans. In the European cases where

success was attributed to mentoring, long-term relationships seemed to be present as well as a strong investment in the success of the manager. This finding would support Hofstede's (1984, 1991; Hofstede & Sami Kassem, 1976) cross-national research comparison of countries on power distance. According to Hofstede, European countries—namely Belgium, France, and Italy—where power distance is greatest would tend to favor hierarchical organizations where absolute power is granted to bosses. For managers to succeed in these organizations, an emotional dependency on their boss would be considered natural and customary to move up in the organization. This is not to say that North Americans who are considered to have low power distance relative to many other countries do not rely on mentoring relationships. In fact, Morrison et al. (1987) found that relationships between the women in their study and their top management were important for success. Their research showed senior management was invested in moving women up into more senior positions where there were previously very few or no women. Today, however, many North Americans may find themselves in organizations that are downsizing, undergoing mergers, and moving to structures that are less hierarchical and more team-based. These managers may in fact have had mentors help along the way, but their ultimate success more likely may be attributed to their individual achievement when the turbulence in their environments is at its greatest.

Third, although the inability to build and lead a team is a theme that can be found in all derailment research, the scope of what it captures is clearly changing over time. In the early interviews, this derailment factor had to do mostly with failing to staff effectively, to hire the right people, or hiring in one's own image. The language of those early interviews was set in the context of traditional hierarchical organizations operating in a relatively stable environment. Yet in recent interviews, both in Europe and the U.S., senior executives place emphasis directly on the building of a productive working (and often diverse) team of people and the effective leadership of that team over time. Again, this shift in language is suggestive of the kinds of changes organizations have made over the past 10 years toward flatter structures and work through teams, and also reflects change in the expected role and capacities required of leaders.

General Discussion

Why Are European and North American Results so Similar?

Whenever the topic is leadership or leadership development, the expectation tends to be that one will see significant differences between studies done with North American managers and studies done with managers in other countries. Surely, differences are found when the issue at hand has to do with national cultural values (Hall, 1981; Hampden-Turner & Trompenaars, 1993; Hofstede, 1984, 1991; Hofstede & Sami Kassem, 1976; Hoppe, 1990; Kim, Triandis, Kagitcibasi, Choi, & Yoon, 1994; Triandis & Bontempo, 1986; Triandis et al., 1990; Trompenaars, 1993) or when the comparison is of managers in the U.S. to managers working in organizations in a very traditional or rural economy.

Yet the leadership requirements in organizations derive at least as much from the nature of the business and from how the organization is structured to do its work as from the dimensions of culture that are rooted in nationality or religion. The economies and business environments forming the working context for European organizations today are in many ways not vastly different from the economies and business environments experienced by U.S. companies, and recent research (Hofstede, 1991; Jaques, 1976; Jaques & Clement, 1991) has shown that both accountability hierarchies and organizational cultures are more alike across organizations in Europe and the U.S. than they are different. Finally, our data suggest that although there are not great differences in factors related to derailment when U.S. and European managers are compared, there are profound differences in those individual values that relate to leadership (as measured by SYMLOG) when successful and derailed managers are compared.

Derailment results from a lack of fit between individual values and development, on the one hand, and organizational values and needs, on the other. And the organizational values and needs of large or multinational companies today do not differ significantly when Europe is compared to the U.S. To the extent that organizations are made up of jobs that successively demand more and different skills and perspectives—and to the extent that organizations the world over are faced with environments and markets that demand of their senior executives interpersonal skills, adaptability, team orientation, and high performance—the dynamics of derailment will not differ dramatically.

This does not mean that a North American manager would not have difficulty if he or she took a position in a large German or French manufacturing firm, for example. That manager might be at high risk of derailment because of the great demand to adapt to the new culture and norms and the need to be seen as interpersonally skilled in a culture one does not completely understand. But the important point is that the interpersonal skills and the ability to adapt would be the critical factors (as called out by the senior executives interviewed in the present research) and not the specific features of the environment (the norms, values, ways of being) that one is asked to adapt to.

Is Derailment Still a Useful Concept?

Derailment is a fact of life in organizations, more today than ever before. Relatively few managers will get beyond general management ranks, either because of lack of fit (skills, development) for more senior-level jobs or due to lack of open positions in increasingly leaner organizations. Downsizing and the move toward the "new employee contract" has added to the likelihood that even competent people will derail.

If organizations continue to move toward more temporary forms and structures, as well as toward new ways of contracting with employees for their skills and contributions, the idea that there is one "track" to the top that all highly competent people should be on may be an outmoded idea. If organizations are becoming boundaryless and taking individuals' careers toward boundarylessness, as well (Mirvis & Hall, 1994), then it may make more sense to think not of a track one falls off but of a network one moves within.

For most managers, the notion that derailment from the "track to the top" is something to be controlled or avoided by the individual or the organization may also be dated. In fact, if organizations are made more adaptable and robust by utilizing the majority of professional employees and managers only as long as there is a fit between their skills and organizational needs, then it may make little sense to design human resources initiatives to prevent derailment for the majority of managers.

Yet we still believe the results of studying derailment are of significant utility for both that portion of the managerial population whose career will continue to proceed up through one organization as well as for the portion that will move between organizations frequently, even when these are mostly lateral moves. A key challenge for both groups is adaptation and personal development in the face of transition. Often a restructuring effort leaves the survivors with jobs of much greater scope, more work to do with fewer resources and increased responsibility. The people let go during a reduction are faced with the challenge of seeing and taking advantage of the opportunity in their situation. To be effective in this set of circumstances probably demands the same positive outlook, interpersonal strength, adaptability, team orientation, and tendency toward persistent hard work seen in managers who succeed within a traditional organization.

Although the key use of derailment research in the past has been to understand the development needed (to prevent derailment) by people as they move up in an organization, at its core derailment really has to do with a failure of fit of the individual with the evolving demands of the job over time (often at successively higher organizational levels). To the extent that derailment research yields understanding of competencies or characteristics that relate to success in jobs with high levels of turbulence, ambiguity, and responsibility, the results remain valuable and probably more useful than ever.

References

Bales, R. F. (1970). *Personality and interpersonal behavior.* New York: Holt, Rinehart, and Winston.

Bales, R. F. (1993). *Bales report on an individual field diagram.* San Diego, CA: SYMLOG Consulting Group.

Ball, R. S. (1983). The predictability of occupational level from intelligence. *Journal of Consulting Psychology, 2,* 184-186.

Bass, B., & Stogdill, R. (Eds.). (1990). *Bass & Stogdill's handbook of leadership: Theory, research, and managerial applications (3rd ed.).* New York: The Free Press.

Blake, R., & Mouton, J. (1985). *The Managerial Grid III.* Houston, TX: Gulf Publishing House.

Cornwell, J. M. (1983). *A meta-analysis of selected trait research in the leadership literature.* Atlanta, GA: Southeastern Psychological Association.

Ekvall, G., & Arvonen, J. (1994). Leadership profiles, situation and effectiveness. *Creativity and Innovation Management, 3,* 139-161.

Fiedler, F. E. (1967). *A theory of leadership effectiveness.* New York: McGraw-Hill.

Fiedler, F. E. (1971). *Leadership.* New York: General Learning Press.

Fleishman, E. (1953). The description of supervisory behavior. *Journal of Applied Psychology, 37,* 1-6.

Gopalan, S. (1991). *An empirical investigation of the relationship between national and organizational cultures in the United States, Brazil, and India.* Unpublished doctoral dissertation, Louisiana Tech University.

Haire, M., Ghiselli, E. E., & Porter, L. W. (1966). *Managerial thinking—An international study.* New York: John Wiley & Sons.

Hall, E. T. (1981). *Beyond culture.* New York: Doubleday.

Hampden-Turner, C., & Trompenaars, A. (1993). *The seven cultures of capitalism: Value systems for creating wealth in the United States, Japan, Germany, France, Britain, Sweden, and the Netherlands* (1st ed.). New York: Currency.

Hersey, P., & Blanchard, K. (1988). *Management of organizational behavior.* New York: Prentice Hall.

Hofstede, G. (1980). *Culture's consequences: International differences in work-related values.* Beverly Hills, CA: Sage.

Hofstede, G. (1990). Measuring organizational cultures: A qualitative and quantitative study across twenty cases. *Administrative Science Quarterly, 35,* 286-316.

Hofstede, G. (1991). *Cultures and organizations.* Berkshire, England: McGraw-Hill.

Hofstede, G., & Sami Kassem, M. (1976). *European contributions to organization theory.* Assen: Van Gorcum.

Hoppe, M. H. (1990). *A comparative study of country elites: International differences in work-related values and learning and their implications for management training and development.* Unpublished doctoral dissertation, The University of North Carolina at Chapel Hill.

Howard, A., & Bray, D. W. (1988). *Managerial lives in transition: Advancing age and changing times.* New York: Guilford Press.

Jaques, E. (1976). *A general theory of bureaucracy.* London: Halsted Press.

Jaques, E., & Clement, S. (1991). *Executive leadership.* New York: Blackwell.

Kaplan, R. E., Drath, W. H., & Kofodimos, J. R. (1991). *Beyond ambition: How driven managers can lead better and live better.* San Francisco, CA: Jossey-Bass.

Kim, U., Triandis, H., Kagitcibasi, C., Choi, S-C., & Yoon, G. (Eds.). (1994). *Individualism and collectivism theory, method, and applications.* Thousand Oaks, CA: Sage.

Kovach, B. (1986, Autumn). The derailment of fast-track managers. *Organizational Dynamics,* pp. 41-48.

Likert, R. (1961). *New patterns of management.* New York: McGraw-Hill.

Lombardo, M., & McCauley, C. (1988). *The dynamics of management derailment.* Greensboro, NC: Center for Creative Leadership.

Lord, R. G., DeVader, C. L., & Alliger, G. M. (1986). A meta-analysis of the relation between personality traits and leadership perceptions: An application of validity generalizations procedures. *Journal of Applied Psychology, 71,* 402-410.

Mann, R. D. (1959). A review of the relationships between personality and performance in small groups. *Psychological Bulletin, 56,* 241-270.

McCall, M. W., Jr., & Lombardo, M. M. (1983). *Off the track: Why and how successful executives get derailed.* Greensboro, NC: Center for Creative Leadership.

Mirvis, P., & Hall, D. T. (1994). Psychological success and the boundaryless career. *Journal of Organizational Behavior, 15,* 365-380.

Morrison, A. M., White, R. P., & Van Velsor, E. (1987). *Breaking the glass ceiling: Can women reach the top of America's largest corporations?* Reading, MA: Addison-Wesley.

Ronen, S., & Kraut, A. I. (1977). Similarities among countries based on employee work values and attitudes. *Columbia Journal of World Business, 12,* 89-96.

Shipper, F., & Dillard, J. (1994). *Comparing the managerial skills of early derailers vs. fast trackers, late derailers vs. long-term fast trackers, and mid-career derailers vs. recoverers.* Paper presented at the annual meeting of the Academy of Management, Dallas, Texas.

Stogdill, R. M. (1948). Personal factors associated with leadership: A survey of the literature. *Journal of Psychology, 25,* 35-71.

Stogdill, R., & Coons, A. (1957). *Leader behavior: Its description and measurement.* Bureau of Business Research, Ohio State University.

Triandis, H. C., & Bontempo, R. (1986). The measurement of the etic aspects of individualism and collectivism across cultures. *Australian Journal of Psychology, 3*(3), 257-267.

Triandis, H. C., McCusker, C., & Hui, C. H. (1990). Multimethod probes of individualism and collectivism. *Journal of Personality & Social Psychology, 59*(5), 1006-1020.

Trompenaars, F. (1993). *Riding the waves of culture.* Great Britain: The Economist Books.

Van Velsor, E., & Leslie, J. B. (1991). *Feedback to managers volume II: A review and comparison of sixteen multi-rater feedback instruments.* Greensboro, NC: Center for Creative Leadership.

Appendix A: Success and Derailment Interview Questions

SECTION 1: CONTRASTS

First let's consider the person who "made it" to the top.

1. Briefly tell us what you know about this person's career (a sketch).

2. How did this person first catch the eye of important managers in the company? What kinds of things did he do that held their attention over the years?

3. What do you see as the critical turning points in the person's career (how did she "earn her wings")?

4. How has he changed significantly over the course of his career?

5. How and when did assessment of this person's potential change over time?

6. Did this person ever make a big mistake and then recover from it? How did she recover?

7. Once this person was recognized as a viable candidate for a high-level job, did he get any special assignments, challenges, or bosses because of his potential?

8. When did she first realize that she was considered to be a candidate for a top job? Did this knowledge have an effect on her? Did the company ever recognize her in a formal way? Did that have any effect?

9. What other people played a significant part in his career success? How?

10. What single thing do you think contributed most to this person's ultimate success in getting to the top?

11. How representative is this person of those who make it to the top in your company? How does she differ from others who make it?

Now let's look at the person who "derailed" (was seen as a high-potential candidate for a top job but failed either to achieve that level or to succeed at that level).

1. Briefly tell us what you know about this person's career (a brief sketch).

2. Obviously this person achieved a great deal in the company, even if he never attained what was hoped by management. What were key events that contributed to that success—what led to this person being seen as high-potential and attaining the level he did?

3. What was the sequence of events that led to derailing from the track to the top jobs?

4. What happened to this person afterward?

5. How representative is this person of others who get derailed? How does she differ from the others who derail?

SECTION 2: OTHER EXPERIENCES

We have dealt with two specific examples, but your experience with high-potential executives is probably broader than that.

1. Can you think of other examples that would help us better understand the road to the top?

    a. Examples of critical career turning points—events that had a significant impact on a person's growth or advancement.

    b. Examples of "fatal flaws"—things that caused high-potential persons to derail along the road to the top.

Appendix B: SYMLOG® Rating Form

Research Survey

You will answer TWO (2) questions on this form. Your responses are strictly confidential. It is NOT necessary to complete the identification section on the other side of this form.

Please answer the following questions describing the same "successful" and "derailed" persons you depicted during the interview.

Question 1. In general, what kinds of values did the SUCCESSFUL leader you described show in his or her behavior?

To answer this question, turn this page over and locate the <u>column</u> labeled CODE NAME 1 SUL. Mark your responses with a <u>No. 2 pencil</u>.

Go **down** the column marking R = Rarely, S = Sometimes, or O = Often for each of the 26 descriptive items. NOT ALL OF THE ITEMS MAY SEEM TO GO TOGETHER. IF EVEN ONE ITEM FITS, USE IT AS YOUR GUIDE.

When you have finished marking all 26 items for Question 1, please answer the following:

Question 2. In general, what kinds of values did the DERAILED leader you described show in his or her behavior?

(Mark your responses down the column labeled CODE NAME 2 DRD.)

	DESCRIPTIVE ITEMS—Individual and Organizational Values	CODE NAME 1 SUL			CODE NAME 2 DRD		
U	1 Individual financial success, personal prominence and power 1	⊂R⊐	⊂S⊐	⊂O⊐	⊂R⊐	⊂S⊐	⊂O⊐
UP	2 Popularity and social success, being liked and admired 2	⊂R⊐	⊂S⊐	⊂O⊐	⊂R⊐	⊂S⊐	⊂O⊐
UPF	3 Active teamwork toward common goals, organizational unity 3	⊂R⊐	⊂S⊐	⊂O⊐	⊂R⊐	⊂S⊐	⊂O⊐
UF	4 Efficiency, strong impartial management 4	⊂R⊐	⊂S⊐	⊂O⊐	⊂R⊐	⊂S⊐	⊂O⊐
UNF	5 Active reinforcement of authority, rules, and regulations 5	⊂R⊐	⊂S⊐	⊂O⊐	⊂R⊐	⊂S⊐	⊂O⊐
UN	6 Tough-minded, self-oriented assertiveness 6	⊂R⊐	⊂S⊐	⊂O⊐	⊂R⊐	⊂S⊐	⊂O⊐
UNB	7 Rugged, self-oriented individualism, resistance to authority 7	⊂R⊐	⊂S⊐	⊂O⊐	⊂R⊐	⊂S⊐	⊂O⊐
UB	8 Having a good time, releasing tension, relaxing control 8	⊂R⊐	⊂S⊐	⊂O⊐	⊂R⊐	⊂S⊐	⊂O⊐
UPB	9 Protecting less able members, providing help when needed 9	⊂R⊐	⊂S⊐	⊂O⊐	⊂R⊐	⊂S⊐	⊂O⊐
P	10 Equality, democratic participation in decision making 10	⊂R⊐	⊂S⊐	⊂O⊐	⊂R⊐	⊂S⊐	⊂O⊐
PF	11 Responsible idealism, collaborative work 11	⊂R⊐	⊂S⊐	⊂O⊐	⊂R⊐	⊂S⊐	⊂O⊐
F	12 Conservative, established, "correct" ways of doing things 12	⊂R⊐	⊂S⊐	⊂O⊐	⊂R⊐	⊂S⊐	⊂O⊐
NF	13 Restraining individual desires for organizational goals 13	⊂R⊐	⊂S⊐	⊂O⊐	⊂R⊐	⊂S⊐	⊂O⊐
N	14 Self-protection, self-interest first, self-sufficiency 14	⊂R⊐	⊂S⊐	⊂O⊐	⊂R⊐	⊂S⊐	⊂O⊐
NB	15 Rejection of established procedures, rejection of conformity 15	⊂R⊐	⊂S⊐	⊂O⊐	⊂R⊐	⊂S⊐	⊂O⊐
B	16 Change to new procedures, different values, creativity 16	⊂R⊐	⊂S⊐	⊂O⊐	⊂R⊐	⊂S⊐	⊂O⊐
PB	17 Friendship, mutual pleasure, recreation 17	⊂R⊐	⊂S⊐	⊂O⊐	⊂R⊐	⊂S⊐	⊂O⊐
DP	18 Trust in the goodness of others............................ 18	⊂R⊐	⊂S⊐	⊂O⊐	⊂R⊐	⊂S⊐	⊂O⊐
DPF	19 Dedication, faithfulness, loyalty to the organization 19	⊂R⊐	⊂S⊐	⊂O⊐	⊂R⊐	⊂S⊐	⊂O⊐
DF	20 Obedience to the chain of command, complying with authority .. 20	⊂R⊐	⊂S⊐	⊂O⊐	⊂R⊐	⊂S⊐	⊂O⊐
DNF	21 Self-sacrifice if necessary to reach organizational goals 21	⊂R⊐	⊂S⊐	⊂O⊐	⊂R⊐	⊂S⊐	⊂O⊐
DN	22 Passive rejection of popularity, going it alone................. 22	⊂R⊐	⊂S⊐	⊂O⊐	⊂R⊐	⊂S⊐	⊂O⊐
DNB	23 Admission of failure, withdrawal of effort 23	⊂R⊐	⊂S⊐	⊂O⊐	⊂R⊐	⊂S⊐	⊂O⊐
DB	24 Passive non-cooperation with authority 24	⊂R⊐	⊂S⊐	⊂O⊐	⊂R⊐	⊂S⊐	⊂O⊐
DPB	25 Quiet contentment, taking it easy 25	⊂R⊐	⊂S⊐	⊂O⊐	⊂R⊐	⊂S⊐	⊂O⊐
D	26 Giving up personal needs and desires, passivity................ 26	⊂R⊐	⊂S⊐	⊂O⊐	⊂R⊐	⊂S⊐	⊂O⊐

R=RARELY S=SOMETIMES O=OFTEN

SYMLOG Consulting Group

18580 Polvera Dr.
San Diego, CA 92128
(619)673-2098

Appendix C: Quantitative Support—SYMLOG® Results

SYMLOG®, under development at Harvard University for the last 45 years, is a comprehensive synthesis of findings, theories, and methods from psychology, social psychology, sociology, economics, political science, and several related disciplines. The theory underlying this instrument is both a "field theory" and a "systems theory." The empirical measurements are designed to take into realistic account the assumption that every pattern of behavior of an individual or a group is organically interlinked with other patterns and with a larger context. The interlinked processes have the properties of a "dynamic field" of interacting and competing tensions (Van Velsor & Leslie, 1991).

SYMLOG is based on a model of group dynamics that measures conflicting tensions that may enhance or inhibit effective leadership and teamwork. According to the theory, people unify around similar values and polarize around dissimilar ones. Three bi-polar dimensions characterize values that can be inferred through behaviors (the instrument items). Each descriptor pair represents opposite ends of a single dimension: (1) Dominance versus Submissiveness, (2) Friendliness versus Unfriendliness, and (3) Acceptance of, versus Opposition to, the Task Orientation of Established Authority.

The Dominance-Submissiveness dimension represents the value or importance perceived to be attached to prominence, power, status, and personal influence of an individual in relation to other group members (Bales, 1970). Dominant members tend to be more highly engaged participants and tend to impose their views on the group. The more submissive members tend to be quiet, passive, and somewhat introverted.

The Friendliness versus Unfriendliness dimension is described by Bales (1970) as being descriptive of values perceived as egalitarian, cooperative, and protective of others. The unfriendly side of the three-dimensional space is associated with values perceived as being self-interested and self-protective.

The Acceptance of, versus Opposition to, the Task Orientation of Established Authority refers to values associated with promoting/following, or creating/changing, rules and procedures (e.g., customs, norms, work demands, written rules, laws, and regulations) set up by authorities external to the work group and who will be responsible for evaluating the work group's performance.

Figures 1 and 2 present the final average location of certain images as rated by a sample of North American and European executives. The field diagram provides a forum to plot the three-dimensional location of the images on a two-dimensional piece of paper. The diagram, broken into four quadrants, presents values on Friendly versus Unfriendly behavior (the P-N line on the diagram) in comparison to the Acceptance of, versus Opposition to, the Task Orientation of Established Authority (the F-B line on the diagram). The third dimension, values on Dominance versus Submissiveness, is represented by the size of the image circles. In this case, there are two image circles: one for the image of successful executives (labeled SUL) and another for the image of derailed executives (labeled DRD). The larger the image circle, the more dominant the image; the smaller the circle, the more submissive values are related to the image.

A very large circle, called the "reference circle," has also been drawn in the top right-hand quadrant of the field diagram. This reference circle represents the area in the field in which individuals (North American and European executives in this study) are likely to share similar values, be drawn to one another, and cooperate well. Within this area is the normative location of the most effective leader or group (represented by the broken image circle labeled MEP—most effective profile). The large "opposition circle," located on the bottom left corner, is the area associated with images of people or fragile coalitions in opposition to the MEP.

Previous research by the SYMLOG Consulting Group reveals that leaders perceived to be at or near the MEP tend to maintain a close average balance among: (1) moderately high activity—initiating many acts with the group as a whole and attracting many acts of initiation and response from individuals; (2) moderately high likability—inspiring a justified liking from many others; and (3) a moderately high, but not aversive, emphasis on task accomplishment—but showing outstanding competence, initiative, and persistence in structuring and performing the tasks of the group, or in persuading and training other members to perform the various roles needed. This often included educating and training others to replace themselves in a leadership role and inducting such members into the role (Bales, 1993).

Members seen in this location have a particular balance of values that is strategic in promoting teamwork. They usually show no excess of either dominance or submissiveness. They place about equal emphasis on task requirements and needs for group integration. They often show an altruistic concern not only for the members of the team or "in-group" but also for the welfare of other individuals and groups. Others tend to describe them as sincerely "good." Their values meet group needs for cooperation and high achievement (Bales, 1993).

As we can see in Figures 1 and 2, SYMLOG clearly differentiates the successful (image circle labeled SUL) from the derailed (image circle labeled DRD) for both North American and European executives. The location of the SUL images suggests successful Europeans and North Americans are close to the most effective profile (MEP) and perceived by their senior executives to place a moderate emphasis on values associated with dominance, acceptance of authority, and being friendly. In other words, the successful executives are likely to behave in an assertive, analytical, task-oriented, problem-solving, egalitarian, cooperative manner while being unconcerned with status differences and disagreement.

There is some similarity too between North American and European derailed executives. As can be seen in the field diagrams, the circles representing the derailed groups' averages are located on the left side, the "values on unfriendly behavior" side of the diagram. This value may be inferred from derailed executives' behavior that seems more "self" centered than "group" centered. In general, these executives are seen as unfriendly and negativistic.

A few subtle differences occur, however, between the derailed Europeans and the North Americans. The derailed Europeans are located below the U.S. derailed executives on the SYMLOG dimension that reflects the acceptance of established authority around tasks. In other words, the derailed European may be perceived as isolated, in opposition to upper management, and in disagreement with others' attempts to preserve solidarity, equality, and common rewards for the good of the group as a whole. There is also a slight difference in the size of the groups' circles. Although this difference is probably insignificant, the derailed European group's circle is a little larger than that of the North American derailed group.

Overall SYMLOG results emphasize the perceptions of the derailed Europeans as domineering and powerful (reflected in the authoritarian theme in our interview data), having excessive dependence upon self (reflected in the "Organizational isolation" theme in our interviews), in opposition to authority (reflected in the "Conflict with upper management" theme in our interview data), and unfriendly (reflected in the interview themes "Poor working relations" and "Inability to build and lead a team"). Two cases from the interview data exemplify the unfriendly, oppositional (SYMLOG) values of a derailer profile:

> He was reluctant to communicate with his hierarchical boss. He was communicating with his boss's boss. He had an enormous ego, therefore he failed to recognize a superior in the most general terms! He had

Figure 1

Group Average Field Diagram
Based on ratings made by the Group

**Based on ratings from European managers
CCL/SYMLOG Success-Derailment Research**

VALUES ON ACCEPTING TASK-ORIENTATION OF ESTABLISHED AUTHORITY

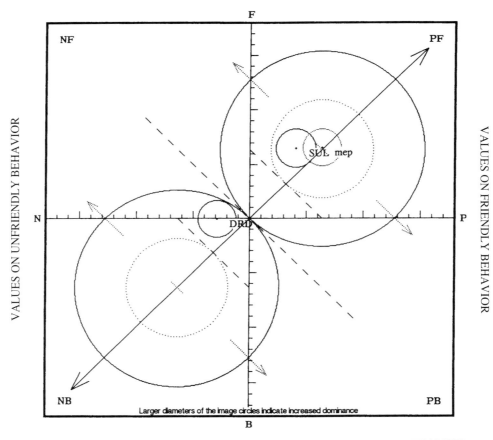

VALUES ON OPPOSING TASK-ORIENTATION OF ESTABLISHED AUTHORITY

Figure 2

Group Average Field Diagram
Based on ratings made by the Group

Based on ratings from U.S. managers
CCL/SYMLOG Success-Derailment Research

VALUES ON ACCEPTING TASK-ORIENTATION OF ESTABLISHED AUTHORITY

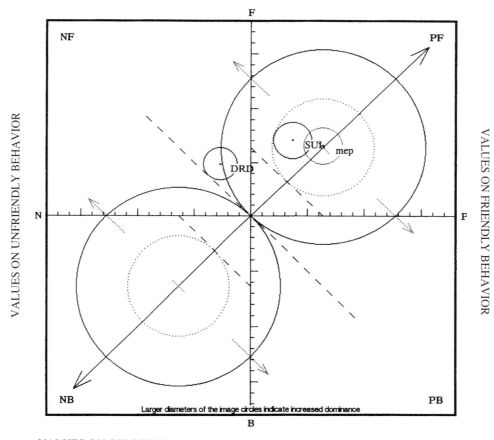

VALUES ON OPPOSING TASK-ORIENTATION OF ESTABLISHED AUTHORITY

SYMLOG Consulting Group 18580 Polvera Dr. San Diego, CA 92128 (619) 673-2098

peculiarities, he exercised in his office and walked around in bare feet. He perceived that everything is allowed for him. He thought of himself as a super manager.

He often used his "big mouth" to make rude statements about the company's policies. He could not cooperate in broad matters. Became negative, wanted to be a "lone wolf."

Similarities and differences between successful and derailed executives can also be seen by comparing bar graphs of the items comprising the three SYMLOG dimensions (see Figures 3-6). The E-line on the bar graph represents the normative profile (MEP plotted on the field diagram).[4] For the most part, successful North Americans and Europeans are similar to the most effective profile which reflects acceptance of authority, friendliness, and moderately dominant behavior (see Figures 3-6). At the item level, successful managers are seen as placing value on dedication to the organization, active teamwork toward common goals, impartiality, collaboration, friendship, protecting less able members, and relaxing control. These SYMLOG scores relate to the interview success themes of building strong collaborative relationships, team building and leadership skills, and ability to adapt. The examples below exemplify successful leaders' SYMLOG profile.

He believed that success can be achieved through democratic work, work whose results could benefit everyone. He is honest, collaborative and open to new ideas. He is a great supporter of his people and his people's ideas. He is accessible to everyone in the company.

He's a dynamic man with tremendous energy and creativity who puts an enormous amount of work into his leadership roles. He's a doer, achievement oriented, he doesn't need sleep. He's an extremely committed company servant.

The derailed executives, for the most part, are rated the opposite of the successful ones (see Figures 5-6). If the bar graph x's for the 26 items are connected (for both North Americans and Europeans), one finds a profile which is the opposite of the most effective profile, i.e., non-acceptance of the established authority around tasks, unfriendly, and submissive behaviors. As was seen in our interview data, derailed managers are seen as placing value on going it alone and being more individualistic. Unlike their successful

Figure 3

Bargraph
Ratings made by the Group on: SUL

Based on ratings from European managers

Type: UF   Final Location: 4.2U   4.OP   6.4F   Raters: 42
the bar of X's = the average rating on each item   E = the "optimum" location for most effective teamwork

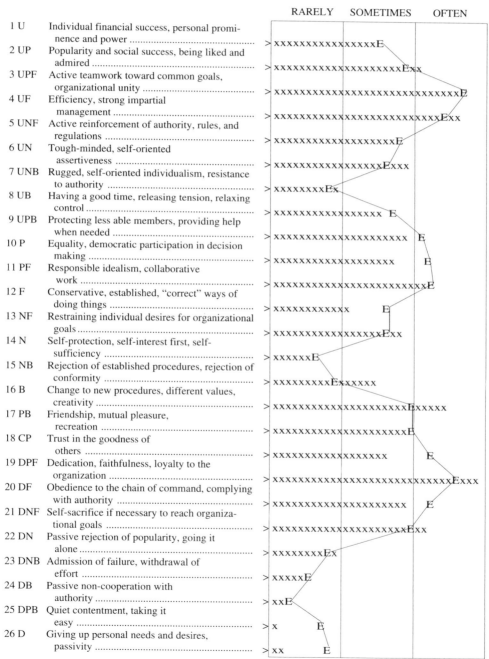

		RARELY	SOMETIMES	OFTEN
1 U	Individual financial success, personal prominence and power	> xxxxxxxxxxxxxxxxxxE		
2 UP	Popularity and social success, being liked and admired	> xxxxxxxxxxxxxxxxxxxxxExx		
3 UPF	Active teamwork toward common goals, organizational unity	> xxxxxxxxxxxxxxxxxxxxxxxxxxxxxxxxxxE		
4 UF	Efficiency, strong impartial management	> xxxxxxxxxxxxxxxxxxxxxxxxxxxxxxxExx		
5 UNF	Active reinforcement of authority, rules, and regulations	> xxxxxxxxxxxxxxxxxxxxxxE		
6 UN	Tough-minded, self-oriented assertiveness	> xxxxxxxxxxxxxxxxxxxExxx		
7 UNB	Rugged, self-oriented individualism, resistance to authority	> xxxxxxxxxEx		
8 UB	Having a good time, releasing tension, relaxing control	> xxxxxxxxxxxxxxxxxxx E		
9 UPB	Protecting less able members, providing help when needed	> xxxxxxxxxxxxxxxxxxxxxx E		
10 P	Equality, democratic participation in decision making	> xxxxxxxxxxxxxxxxxxxx	E	
11 PF	Responsible idealism, collaborative work	> xxxxxxxxxxxxxxxxxxxxxxxxxxxxxxxE		
12 F	Conservative, established, "correct" ways of doing things	> xxxxxxxxxxxxxx	E	
13 NF	Restraining individual desires for organizational goals	> xxxxxxxxxxxxxxxxxxxxExx		
14 N	Self-protection, self-interest first, self-sufficiency	> xxxxxxE		
15 NB	Rejection of established procedures, rejection of conformity	> xxxxxxxxxxExxxxxx		
16 B	Change to new procedures, different values, creativity	> xxxxxxxxxxxxxxxxxxxxxxxxxxxxExxxxx		
17 PB	Friendship, mutual pleasure, recreation	> xxxxxxxxxxxxxxxxxxxxxxxxxE		
18 CP	Trust in the goodness of others	> xxxxxxxxxxxxxxxxxx	E	
19 DPF	Dedication, faithfulness, loyalty to the organization	> xxxxxxxxxxxxxxxxxxxxxxxxxxxxxxxxxxxExxx		
20 DF	Obedience to the chain of command, complying with authority	> xxxxxxxxxxxxxxxxxxxxxx	E	
21 DNF	Self-sacrifice if necessary to reach organizational goals	> xxxxxxxxxxxxxxxxxxxxxxxxxxExx		
22 DN	Passive rejection of popularity, going it alone	> xxxxxxxxxEx		
23 DNB	Admission of failure, withdrawal of effort	> xxxxxxE		
24 DB	Passive non-cooperation with authority	> xxE		
25 DPB	Quiet contentment, taking it easy	> x	E	
26 D	Giving up personal needs and desires, passivity	> xx	E	

Figure 4

Bargraph
Ratings made by the Group on: SUL

Based on ratings from U.S. managers

Type: F   Final Location: 2.8U   3.7P   7.0F   Raters: 20
the bar of X's = the average rating on each item   E = the "optimum" location for most effective teamwork

		RARELY	SOMETIMES	OFTEN

1 U	Individual financial success, personal prominence and power	> xxxxxxxxxxxxxxxxxxExxxx
2 UP	Popularity and social success, being liked and admired	> xxxxxxxxxxxxxxxxxxxxE
3 UPF	Active teamwork toward common goals, organizational unity	> xxxxxxxxxxxxxxxxxxxxxxxxxxxxxxx E
4 UF	Efficiency, strong impartial management	> xxxxxxxxxxxxxxxxxxxxxxxxxxxxxxxxxEx
5 UNF	Active reinforcement of authority, rules, and regulations	> xxxxxxxxxxxxxxxxxxxxxE
6 UN	Tough-minded, self-oriented assertiveness	> xxxxxxxxxxxxxxxxxxExxxxxx
7 UNB	Rugged, self-oriented individualism, resistance to authority	> xxxxxxxxExxxxx
8 UB	Having a good time, releasing tension, relaxing control	> xxxxxxxxxxxxxxxxxxxxE
9 UPB	Protecting less able members, providing help when needed	> xxxxxxxxxxxxxxxxxxxxxxxxxE
10 P	Equality, democratic participation in decision making	> xxxxxxxxxxxxxxxxxxxxxxxxxxE
11 PF	Responsible idealism, collaborative work	> xxxxxxxxxxxxxxxxxxxxxxxxxxxxxxxxExxx
12 F	Conservative, established, "correct" ways of doing things	> xxxxxxxxxxxxxxxxx E
13 NF	Restraining individual desires for organizational goals	> xxxxxxxxxxxxxxxxxxxxExxxxx
14 N	Self-protection, self-interest first, self-sufficiency	> xxxxxxExxx
15 NB	Rejection of established procedures, rejection of conformity	> xxxxxxxxxxExx
16 B	Change to new procedures, different values, creativity	> xxxxxxxxxxxxxxxxxxxxxxxxxxxExxxx
17 PB	Friendship, mutual pleasure, recreation	> xxxxxxxxxxxxxxxxxxx E
18 CP	Trust in the goodness of others	> xxxxxxxxxxxxxxxxxxxxxxxxxxxxxExx
19 DPF	Dedication, faithfulness, loyalty to the organization	> xxxxxxxxxxxxxxxxxxxxxxxxxxxxxxxxxxxxExx
20 DF	Obedience to the chain of command, complying with authority	> xxxxxxxxxxxxxxxxxxxxxxxxxxxE
21 DNF	Self-sacrifice if necessary to reach organizational goals	> xxxxxxxxxxxxxxxxxxxxxxxxxxxxExxxxx
22 DN	Passive rejection of popularity, going it alone	> xxxxxxxxExxxxxxxxx
23 DNB	Admission of failure, withdrawal of effort	> xxxxxE
24 DB	Passive non-cooperation with authority	> xxExxxx
25 DPB	Quiet contentment, taking it easy	> xx E
26 D	Giving up personal needs and desires, passivity	> xxxxxxxxExx

Figure 5

Bargraph
Ratings made by the Group on: DRD

Based on ratings from European managers

Type: AVE Final Location: 2.8U 3.0N 0.2B Raters: 42
the bar of X's = the average rating on each item E = the "optimum" location for most effective teamwork

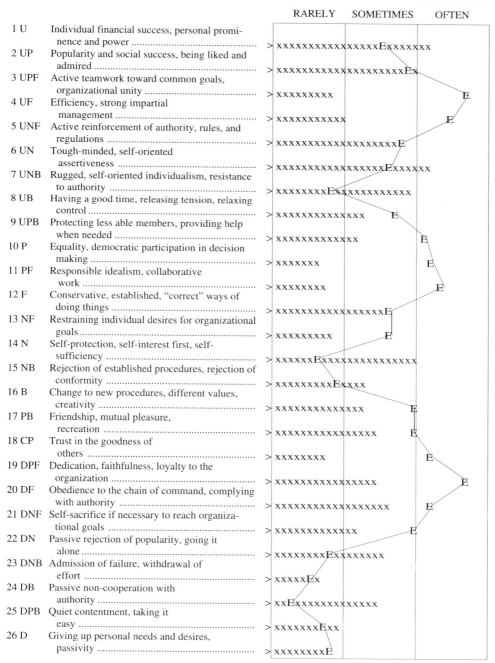

		RARELY	SOMETIMES	OFTEN
1 U	Individual financial success, personal prominence and power			
2 UP	Popularity and social success, being liked and admired			
3 UPF	Active teamwork toward common goals, organizational unity			
4 UF	Efficiency, strong impartial management			
5 UNF	Active reinforcement of authority, rules, and regulations			
6 UN	Tough-minded, self-oriented assertiveness			
7 UNB	Rugged, self-oriented individualism, resistance to authority			
8 UB	Having a good time, releasing tension, relaxing control			
9 UPB	Protecting less able members, providing help when needed			
10 P	Equality, democratic participation in decision making			
11 PF	Responsible idealism, collaborative work			
12 F	Conservative, established, "correct" ways of doing things			
13 NF	Restraining individual desires for organizational goals			
14 N	Self-protection, self-interest first, self-sufficiency			
15 NB	Rejection of established procedures, rejection of conformity			
16 B	Change to new procedures, different values, creativity			
17 PB	Friendship, mutual pleasure, recreation			
18 CP	Trust in the goodness of others			
19 DPF	Dedication, faithfulness, loyalty to the organization			
20 DF	Obedience to the chain of command, complying with authority			
21 DNF	Self-sacrifice if necessary to reach organizational goals			
22 DN	Passive rejection of popularity, going it alone			
23 DNB	Admission of failure, withdrawal of effort			
24 DB	Passive non-cooperation with authority			
25 DPB	Quiet contentment, taking it easy			
26 D	Giving up personal needs and desires, passivity			

Figure 6

Bargraph
Ratings made by the Group on: DRD

Based on ratings from U.S. managers

Type: F   Final Location: 0.5U   2.7N   4.9F   Raters: 20
the bar of X's = the average rating on each item   E = the "optimum" location for most effective teamwork

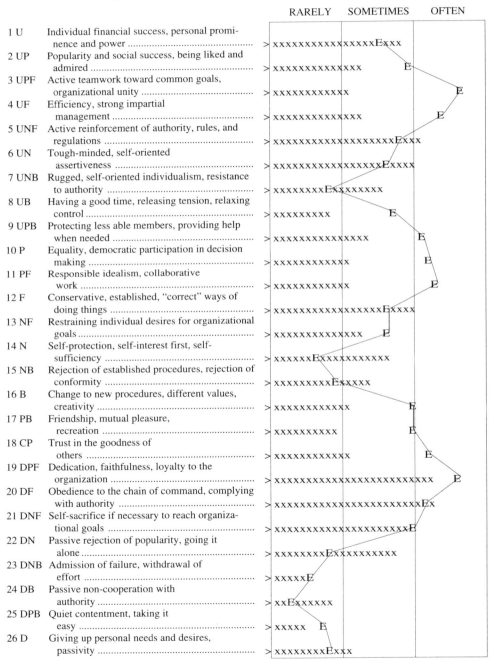

		RARELY	SOMETIMES	OFTEN
1 U	Individual financial success, personal prominence and power	> xxxxxxxxxxxxxxxxxExxx		
2 UP	Popularity and social success, being liked and admired	> xxxxxxxxxxxxxxx	E	
3 UPF	Active teamwork toward common goals, organizational unity	> xxxxxxxxxxxxx		E
4 UF	Efficiency, strong impartial management	> xxxxxxxxxxxxxxxx		E
5 UNF	Active reinforcement of authority, rules, and regulations	> xxxxxxxxxxxxxxxxxxxxxxExxx		
6 UN	Tough-minded, self-oriented assertiveness	> xxxxxxxxxxxxxxxxxxxExxxx		
7 UNB	Rugged, self-oriented individualism, resistance to authority	> xxxxxxxxExxxxxxxx		
8 UB	Having a good time, releasing tension, relaxing control	> xxxxxxxxx	E	
9 UPB	Protecting less able members, providing help when needed	> xxxxxxxxxxxxxxxx	E	
10 P	Equality, democratic participation in decision making	> xxxxxxxxxxxx		E
11 PF	Responsible idealism, collaborative work	> xxxxxxxxxxxxx		E
12 F	Conservative, established, "correct" ways of doing things	> xxxxxxxxxxxxxxxxxxxExxxx		
13 NF	Restraining individual desires for organizational goals	> xxxxxxxxxxxxxxx	E	
14 N	Self-protection, self-interest first, self-sufficiency	> xxxxxxExxxxxxxxxxx		
15 NB	Rejection of established procedures, rejection of conformity	> xxxxxxxxxExxxxxx		
16 B	Change to new procedures, different values, creativity	> xxxxxxxxxxxx	E	
17 PB	Friendship, mutual pleasure, recreation	> xxxxxxxxx	E	
18 CP	Trust in the goodness of others	> xxxxxxxxxxxx	E	
19 DPF	Dedication, faithfulness, loyalty to the organization	> xxxxxxxxxxxxxxxxxxxxxxxxxx		E
20 DF	Obedience to the chain of command, complying with authority	> xxxxxxxxxxxxxxxxxxxxxxxxxxxExx		
21 DNF	Self-sacrifice if necessary to reach organizational goals	> xxxxxxxxxxxxxxxxxxxxxxxE		
22 DN	Passive rejection of popularity, going it alone	> xxxxxxxxExxxxxxxxxx		
23 DNB	Admission of failure, withdrawal of effort	> xxxxxE		
24 DB	Passive non-cooperation with authority	> xxExxxxxxx		
25 DPB	Quiet contentment, taking it easy	> xxxxx E		
26 D	Giving up personal needs and desires, passivity	> xxxxxxxxExxx		

counterparts, they appear to behave as if they do not value teamwork, impartiality, relaxing control, protecting less able members, democratic decision making, collaboration, creativity, friendship, trust in others, or even being liked themselves!

Appendix D: Derailment Factors Most Frequently Mentioned by
North American Senior Executives
(Number of Cases = 20)

Derailment Factor	*Percentage of Cases*
1. Inability to develop or adapt	60
2. Poor working relations	50
3. Inability to build and lead a team	40
4. Poor performance	30
5. Authoritarian	30
6. Too narrow functional orientation	20
7. Too ambitious	15
8. Not prepared for promotion	10
9. Conflict with upper management	10

1. Inability to develop or adapt. The most frequently cited reason for derailment among North American executives is the inability to develop or adapt. For several of these North Americans (33%), the inability to change management style was a factor in their downfall. Others seemed stubborn or resistant to the point where they couldn't change.

2. Poor working relations. It is of no surprise that poor working relationships tops the list of reasons for derailment. In 50% of the cases, this factor was cited. These managers had difficulty with communicating, listening, trusting, and being a team player.

3. Inability to build and lead a team. The inability to lead people during organizational change described the context of 63% of the derailed North Americans.

4. Poor performance. At first glance, it is difficult to believe that managers who make it to at least the general management level derail due to poor performance. We, however, found that poor performance was associated with the derailment of 30% of the cases.

> He had very disappointing results. His very senior level position was a make or break position but he could not produce results.

We had a huge project—our biggest. It is late. It has cost hundreds of thousands of dollars because we didn't have needed staff, and systems, in time. This is her responsibility.

5. Authoritarian. Authoritarian management styles may help managers to succeed in earlier phases of their careers. Our data suggest, however, that it can lead to derailment in the latter years. Senior executives described managers whose authoritarian style succeeded when the organization's top management prescribed to a similar style. As times changed, however, these managers seemed unable to adjust their style to a more participative, empowering one. As a result, these managers were fired, forced to leave the organization, or plateaued.

6. Too narrow functional orientation. Achieving results and moving up in a single organizational function is not an uncommon promotional pattern in organizations. All of the derailed managers with this flaw were successful in their function, but once they moved into a more general management position were unable to "wear multiple hats." One North American senior executive offers us this example:

> She was unable to transition from technical to GM. She has been an *extremely* successful manager in her function. She gets repeated counseling to get the big picture and forget the detail. She does not see her role as strategic.

Additional derailment factors. Relatively few senior executives noted managers' ambition (15%) or drive to succeed as a reason for derailment. Those few that did spoke of executives who presented themselves as capable of more than they actually were. A senior executive noted:

> He was driven to achieve, was ambitious and then he ultimately was not able to deliver.

Ten percent of the senior executives noted a lack of preparation for promotion to be a factor in executive derailment. For example:

> He was put into a position that he was not really suited for. He is better at a technical position rather than management. Just because a person excels at a technical level does not make them a good manager.

"Conflict with upper management" was also cited as a derailment factor in 10% of the cases. These managers seemed to have an antagonist relationship with senior management.

Appendix E: Success Factors Most Frequently Mentioned by North American Senior Executives
(Number of Cases = 20)

Success Factor	*Percentage of Cases*
1. Ability to develop or adapt	55
2. Establishes strong collaborative relationships	50
3. Intelligent	50
4. Consistent exceptional performance	45
5. Strong communicator	45
6. Strategic and visionary	40
7. Ability to build and lead a team	40
8. Business and technical expertise	35
9. Non-authoritarian	25
10. Willingness to take risks	25
11. Problem-solver and entrepreneurial	20
12. Ambitious	15
13. Integrity	15
14. Skilled at managing upward	15

1. Ability to develop or adapt. The most frequently mentioned success factor of North American managers is the ability to develop or adapt. Learning for several of the managers was framed in terms of "maturing over time" and "growing" as the job or organization expanded. Change often occurred as a result of direct feedback.

2. Establishes strong collaborative relationships. Half of the senior executives noted the ability to work with others as important for success. Within these data we can find hints of how these successful managers interacted with others. The senior executives described leaders as enhancing good relationships by sending people cards on their birthdays, listening, supporting others' ideas, and making themselves available to help. They also described successful leaders as "team players."

3. Intelligent. Senior executives attributed leaders' success to their "intelligence," "high IQ," or "brilliance."

4. Consistent exceptional performance. Consistent exceptional performance does make a difference. The successful managers were able to perform their jobs early in their careers and continued to "deliver" throughout their careers. They were described by the senior executives as having "excellent track records," "results oriented," "produces desired outcomes," and "able to get things done."

5. Strong communicator. Leaders' ability to persuade, articulate complex ideas clearly, and communicate expectations were important for North American managers' success.

> He has good presentation skills, polished, smooth presentation, quick on his feet.

6. Strategic and visionary. Many of the senior executives mentioned leaders' ability to analyze complex situations and apply strategic solutions, and their ability to predict future trends and needs as factors contributing to their success. They, for example, described strategic and visionary leaders as ". . . forward looking. He recognized where a change was coming," and, "He is a visionary, he uses his skills to set a mission and figures out ways to charge ahead."

7. Ability to build and lead a team. North American senior executives noted successful leaders' ability to build and lead a team. These managers tended to mentor good people along, set clear goals and let others know what is expected of them, posses the ability to motivate others to reach their goals, and learned over time to surround themselves with people who could compensate for their weaknesses.

> He pitches in, he is a team player. He spends more time with people at work than family because he thinks that it is important that everyone gets along and enjoys work. He tries to create an environment that is pleasant and enjoyable. His philosophy is to treat others as he wants to be treated with promotions. He thinks of "is this how I want to be treated?" He respects people regardless of differences.

8. Business and technical expertise. Demonstrating technical competence and knowledge of the business often got the successful managers in this research noticed and helped them to achieve quality results time and time again.

9. Non-authoritarian. North American senior executives mentioned leaders' non-authoritarian style of management and willingness to take risks as a factor contributing to success. Non-authoritarian leaders empowered others to share their ideas, listen, and embrace diversity. One senior executive referred to her organization's successful leader as one who "lets people grow their own garden. He will let people do what they need to achieve the organization's goals."

10. Willingness to take risks. Successful leaders are also seen by senior executives as willing to take risks in the face of failure.

11. Problem-solver and entrepreneurial. Leaders' ability to solve problems and entrepreneurial skills was a factor for success. A senior executive noted, "He worked outside of the box. He was very creative."

Additional success factors. Eighteen percent of the senior executives mentioned successful leaders as "Ambitious," having "Integrity," and being "Skilled at managing upward." Ambitious describes leaders' drive and determination to make it to the top of their organizations. For these managers, ambition was an asset that didn't interfere with their interpersonal relationships with others. One senior executive offered this insight:

> He has a strong personal ambition but does not let it get in the way of the team, he makes decisions that are best for the company.

Integrity was most often defined as straightforward and following through on promises. The successful North Americans, like their European counterparts, were skilled at managing upward. A senior executive offered this example:

> He was very politically savvy. He could sell what he wanted to which is particularly hard in this matrix organization.

Appendix F: Derailment Factors Most Frequently Mentioned by European Senior Executives
(Number of Cases = 42)

Derailment Factor	*Percentage of Cases*
1. Poor working relations	64
2. Inability to develop or adapt	62
3. Inability to build and lead a team	24
4.. Not prepared for promotion	18
5. Too ambitious	18
6. Poor performance	16
7. Authoritarian	16
8. Too narrow functional orientation	13
9. Conflict with upper management	13
10. Organizational isolation	13

1. Poor working relations. One of the two most frequently mentioned derailment factors involves poor relationships. Managers who possessed this "fatal" characteristic were described as insensitive, manipulative, critical, demanding, and not trustworthy. Other managers lacked a teamwork orientation. Senior executives described them as being solitary, a "lone wolf," not a team player; the inability to communicate was emphasized.

2. Inability to develop or adapt. Many of the European senior executives cited examples of managers' inability to adapt, inflexibility, and narcissism as reasons for derailment. "Absolutely egotistical" and "pig-headed" were commonly used descriptions of flaws that kept managers from changing. In many of the cases, the senior executives gave the managers feedback on areas for improvement. For whatever reason, the derailed managers were unable to learn from feedback and apply the recommendations.

Resistance to cultural change or the inability to adapt to the habits and culture of the company was another common description of this flaw. For some of these managers, company culture changed with mergers. Other managers had difficulty adjusting to another country's culture.

3. Inability to build and lead a team. No "human skills" and "bad people management" were characteristic of about one in four flaws of the European derailed case studies. An example of a senior executive's perception of managers' inability to manage people is provided below.

> He burnt his team. Not only overworked, but psychologically. He did not support people: used people and minimized their work and their contributions, making them feel that they were only a meaningless part of the work. People became more and more reluctant to work with him. He became isolated. Tried to use his power to threaten them. Took more than two years to fire him.

4. Not prepared for promotion. Lack of preparation for a job was another factor mentioned as a reason for derailment. The derailed managers were commonly described as "not prepared for the promotion," "showing a lack of competence in complex tasks," and having "exceeded their level of potential." Sometimes the managers appeared to have taken the initiative that led to the job from which they derailed:

> It seems that people come off the track because they reach or exceed their level of potential. They get so far and then they don't make a success of a job and they are moved sideways rather than bumped out of the door. That happened to this man. But this man judged wrongly: he took on things he didn't have an aptitude for and he was exposed to a manager he found difficult to cope with.

5. Too ambitious. Arrogance, being "too ambitious," "self-promoting without the performance to support," and "over-confident" were also often cited by senior executives as fatal flaws.

6. Not living up to potential. A few managers were reported to have "no gut feeling for job or product," a "lack of drive or hard work." In general, the managers who possessed this fatal flaw had proven themselves incapable of achieving results. The bulk of managers who fell into this category were middle-level managers who were identified as high-potentials but were in the process of derailing because they were not living up to their predicted potential.

Never had he proved himself capable of results, but for six years he managed to stay and get promoted. After two years as Product Manager, he looked for a new job because there they did not accept a period longer than two years without results.

7. Authoritarian. Senior executives noted managers' authoritarian management style to be a factor of their derailment. These managers were characterized as ruling by fear and being dictatorial.

He stopped delegating and became the only central decision-maker. He tried to centralize only around him. He became a dictator.

8. Too narrow functional orientation. A lack of depth or "too narrow a functional orientation" was mentioned in the derailment cases. Many of the managers who possessed this fatal flaw had moved up the organizational ladder in the same functional area (e.g., marketing). When they were given the responsibility for much broader cross-functional areas of the organization, they derailed. One European senior executive described a situation:

He was promoted to director because there was nobody else to take the position at the time. His analysis was very limited. Made major mistakes and flops. He was not competent enough for the position.

9. Conflict with upper management. "Conflict with upper management" was cited as a derailment factor among the Europeans in this research. The majority of these managers did not agree with their boss(es) and were critical of their choices.

He showed impatience, too much impatience, and bumped up against his boss regarding business strategy.

10. Organizational isolation. Senior executives mentioned organizational isolation or "emphasizing boundaries" as fatal flaws. One extreme case was described by an interviewee:

People were quitting or requesting transfers. She expected complete loyalty, to the extreme. She was dictatorial, overly protective of the group and her own ideas which she forced onto the group. Once someone left, she barely said hello to them after that, and their accomplishments were forgotten. . . . She tried to isolate the team almost completely from the other departments and the outside world. Cutting all the links. That way her people couldn't learn about how other units functioned, how other managers behaved.

Appendix G: Success Factors Most Frequently Mentioned by European Senior Executives
(Number of Cases = 42)

Success Factor	*Percentage of Cases*
1. Ability to develop or adapt	67
2. Consistent exceptional performance	57
3. Establishes strong collaborative relationships	57
4. Business and technical expertise	52
5. Problem-solver and entrepreneurial	45
6. Intelligent	43
7. Strong communicator	38
8. Works hard	36
9. Ambitious	29
10. Integrity	26
11. Ability to build and lead a team	24
12. Non-authoritarian	24
13. Skilled at managing upward	21
14. Strategic and visionary	21
15. Has a strong mentor	19
16. Presents a positive self-image	14
17. Willingness to take risks	12
18. Customer orientation	12

1. Ability to develop or adapt. Managers' willingness to develop or adapt is the success factor most often cited by European senior executives. The type of learning spanned several areas such as learning the business, learning from mistakes, learning from direct feedback, and learning that specifically enhances self-development. Many of the successful managers possessed the ability to learn from mistakes, adapt, and move on. The development of several of these managers was described as "having matured." Senior executives referred to them as becoming "more relaxed," "more flexible," "self-controlling," and "more self-assured" over time.

2. Consistent exceptional performance. Early on, "the ability to perform the job" and be "results oriented" was often a factor that initially caught the eye of upper management. For most of these managers, the highest level of performance remained a factor throughout their careers.

3. Establishes strong collaborative relationships. Senior executives mentioned good relationships with bosses, peers, and subordinates as common factors for success. These managers enhance good working relations by sharing responsibility, taking down barriers between people, thanking the people they work with, supporting others' ideas, and being available to discuss problems. Senior executives also described good working relations of successful leaders as "good team members" and a "team player."

4. Business and technical expertise. Over half of the European senior executives attributed managers' early success to their business or technical expertise. These managers were skilled at both the technical and people side of the business.

5. Problem-solver and entrepreneurial. Many of the successful European managers were reported to be persistent, problem-solvers, creative, and successful in implementing new procedures. It was not uncommon to find this particular factor mentioned as a characteristic that contributed to managers being recognized early in their careers by senior management.

6. Intelligent. European senior executives noted successful leaders as "extremely intelligent," "bright," "able to understand a complex situation," and "very fast intellectually."

7. Strong communicator. Many of the successful leaders were described as having the ability to communicate, sell, persuade, negotiate, and state complex problems simply. A senior executive offered this example:

> He likes to seduce, sell and convince. His communication skills are very good.

8. Works hard. Success for Europeans was attributed to working hard and dedication to the work. It was not uncommon for the senior executives to describe the successful leaders as "completely devoted to work," "extremely hard working," "a workaholic," and one who "achieved results by working hard."

9. Ambitious. A strong drive to get to the top of the organization was commonly mentioned as characteristic of the European successful managers.

10. Integrity. Successful managers were seen as exceptionally honest, trustworthy, straightforward, and generally ethical in their behavior. These managers' success was often characterized by terms like "able to gain trust of clients," "always kept promises," and "was trustworthy." One European senior executive offered this unique example:

> He had a good sense of justice, both in respect to himself and others. He once refused a salary increase when he wasn't able to give a salary increase to his people because of a wage freeze.

11. Ability to build and lead a team. Senior executives noted successful leaders' ability to build and lead a team through their encouragement, involvement, empowerment, and motivation of other team members.

> He built a team around him who could work together and produce results. His success depended on that. He hired people who could not only do the job but who could work together.

12. Non-authoritarian. Senior executives also described successful leaders as open to others' ideas and cultures, tolerant, and able to listen to others without manipulating them. In general, these managers used a non-authoritarian style of leadership with their co-workers.

> He managed people by leaving them space to act without jumping on them. He convinced people in a non-authoritarian way. He acted more as their coach.

13. Skilled at managing upward. European managers' success was attributed to the skillful use of influence tactics with more senior executives. These managers managed upward well, lobbied within their organizations, and were generally skillful at getting what they needed from others.

> He was good at taking care of his relationships with superiors. He is good at taking care of people who will be useful for his career. This behavior is necessary in a very big organization, you have to be a political person. Obviously he was good at his job! But he also attended to his career.

14. Strategic and visionary. Strategic and visionary abilities were noted by senior executives as characteristic of the successful European manager. These managers showed abilities to analyze complex situations and apply strategic solutions. Their strategic abilities often made them "visionaries" in anticipating trends and future needs.

> His strategic thinking and having a vision of where we ought to be and what we should be doing is the single thing that contributed most to this person's success.

15. Has a strong mentor. Having a strong advocate or mentor was mentioned as a factor for European managers' success. Many of the managers' bosses or top management served as "role models," "educators," and "counselors." In many of the cases where "mentoring" was specifically mentioned, long-term relationships seemed to be present as well as a strong investment in the success of the manager. For example:

> He was quickly taken into confidence by a VP—that helped his career. . . . That VP always followed the career of our guy and looked out for him as his mentor.

16. Presents a positive self-image. "Presents a good self-image," "confident," and "believes in self" were commonly used terms to describe successful European leaders. One senior executive emphasized confidence as a major factor of success:

> As a young manager, his success came from his belief in himself.

17. Willingness to take risks. Senior executives made reference to managers' willingness to take risks. The risks primarily centered around taking on new jobs or tasks but also included moving themselves and families to other countries.

18. Customer orientation. Successful leaders in our study "understand the customer," "take good care of clients," and "know how to develop better relationships with customers." One European senior executive said of a successful manager's customer orientation:

> He knew how to develop better relationships with customers, through personal relationships and extended contact with the customer.

Appendix H: Limitations

CCL's derailment studies have produced useful results. There are, however, several methodological issues involved with conducting this type of retrospective, qualitative research. All findings are based on senior executives' perceptions. After-the-fact, interviewees may see the derailed as distinguishably different from the successful, although this may not have been the case prior to derailment. Ambition or being ambitious was, for example, reported to be a success factor by many of the European and North American senior executives interviewed. Being *too* ambitious, was, however, reported to be a derailment factor. The same term once used positively may have been applied as an evaluative device (source of failure) only after it was obvious that the manager derailed. We also have no way of knowing that the interviewees' perceptions are completely accurate. We do know, however, that many of the senior executives interviewed played a role in the personnel and career decisions of the people they described. Their perceptions, therefore, have become reality for many of the leaders whose careers they unfolded for the interviewers.

Qualitative or interview-based research is a means of collecting data firsthand on salient aspects of leadership or effectiveness. Although qualitative data can have a richness lacking in quantitative measurement techniques, it can lack the precision (or appearance of precision) found in instruments. As a result of this concern, we incorporated into our more recent research design a means of comparing results using two methods. At the conclusion of each face-to-face interview on success and derailment, we asked the interviewee to complete a SYMLOG® form on the success case they had described, as well as on the case of a derailed executive. Comparing the SYMLOG profiles of the successful and derailed managers allows us to better understand the meaning of both the qualitative and the quantitative results presented here. SYMLOG findings are presented in Appendix C.

Notes

1. The perceived quality of the university may have been mentioned in these interviews because the interviewer, although often bilingual, was usually not of the same national origin as the interviewee.

2. There are also great similarities, over time and across U.S. and E.U. companies, in why derailed managers were seen as successful in the first place. As in the earliest derailment research reported by McCall and Lombardo (1983), executives in Europe who recently derailed were seen as having strong business or technical expertise early on, as being exceptionally intelligent and strong communicators and problem-solvers. Derailed managers in the U.S. 1994 sample were seen as successful early on because of their intelligence, polished self-presentation, business and technical expertise, hard work, and ability to motivate others.

3. Small differences in percentages are not discussed in this paper because of the small sample sizes in most of the interview studies.

4. Research shows that five or more x's (frequency of responses) to the left of the E-line is statistically significant.

CENTER FOR CREATIVE LEADERSHIP PUBLICATIONS

SELECTED REPORTS:

Beyond Work-Family Programs J.R. Kofodimos (1995, Stock #167) $25.00

CEO Selection: A Street-Smart Review G.P. Hollenbeck (1994, Stock #164) $25.00

Coping With an Intolerable Boss M.M. Lombardo & M.W. McCall, Jr. (1984, Stock #305) $10.00

The Creative Opportunists: Conversations with the CEOs of Small Businesses
J.S. Bruce (1992, Stock #316) $12.00

Creativity in the R&D Laboratory T.M. Amabile & S.S. Gryskiewicz (1987, Stock #130) $12.00

**Eighty-eight Assignments for Development in Place: Enhancing the Developmental
Challenge of Existing Jobs** M.M. Lombardo & R.W. Eichinger (1989, Stock #136) $15.00

**Enhancing 360-degree Feedback for Senior Executives: How to Maximize the Benefits and
Minimize the Risks** R.E. Kaplan & C.J. Palus (1994, Stock #160) $15.00

An Evaluation of the Outcomes of a Leadership Development Program C.D. McCauley &
M.W. Hughes-James (1994, Stock #163) $35.00

Evolving Leaders: A Model for Promoting Leadership Development in Programs C.J. Palus &
W.H. Drath (1995, Stock #165) $20.00

Feedback to Managers, Volume I: A Guide to Evaluating Multi-rater Feedback Instruments
E. Van Velsor & J. Brittain Leslie (1991, Stock #149) $20.00

**Feedback to Managers, Volume II: A Review and Comparison of Sixteen Multi-rater
Feedback Instruments** E. Van Velsor & J. Brittain Leslie (1991, Stock #150) $80.00

**Gender Differences in the Development of Managers: How Women Managers Learn From
Experience** E. Van Velsor & M. W. Hughes (1990, Stock #145) $35.00

A Glass Ceiling Survey: Benchmarking Barriers and Practices A.M. Morrison, C.T. Schreiber,
& K.F. Price (1995, Stock #161) $20.00

High Hurdles: The Challenge of Executive Self-Development R.E. Kaplan, W.H. Drath, &
J.R. Kofodimos (1985, Stock #125) $15.00

The Intuitive Pragmatists: Conversations with Chief Executive Officers J.S. Bruce
(1986, Stock #310) $12.00

Key Events in Executives' Lives E.H. Lindsey, V. Homes, & M.W. McCall, Jr.
(1987, Stock #132) $65.00

Leadership for Turbulent Times L.R. Sayles (1995, Stock #325) $20.00

Learning How to Learn From Experience: Impact of Stress and Coping K.A. Bunker &
A.D. Webb (1992, Stock #154) $30.00

A Look at Derailment Today: North America and Europe J. Brittain Leslie & E. Van Velsor
(1996, Stock #169) $25.00

Making Common Sense: Leadership as Meaning-making in a Community of Practice
W.H. Drath & C.J. Palus (1994, Stock #156) $15.00

Managerial Promotion: The Dynamics for Men and Women M.N. Ruderman, P.J. Ohlott, &
K.E. Kram (1996, Stock #170) $15.00

Off the Track: Why and How Successful Executives Get Derailed M.W. McCall, Jr., &
M.M. Lombardo (1983, Stock #121) $10.00

Preventing Derailment: What To Do Before It's Too Late M.M. Lombardo &
R.W. Eichinger (1989, Stock #138) $25.00

The Realities of Management Promotion M.N. Ruderman & P.J. Ohlott (1994, Stock #157) $20.00

**Redefining What's Essential to Business Performance: Pathways to Productivity,
Quality, and Service** L.R. Sayles (1990, Stock #142) $20.00

Succession Planning L.J. Eastman (1995, Stock #324) $20.00

Training for Action: A New Approach to Executive Development R.M. Burnside &
V.A. Guthrie (1992, Stock #153) $15.00

Traps and Pitfalls in the Judgment of Executive Potential M.N. Ruderman & P.J. Ohlott
(1990, Stock #141) $20.00

Twenty-two Ways to Develop Leadership in Staff Managers R.W. Eichinger & M.M. Lombardo
(1990, Stock #144) $15.00

Upward-communication Programs in American Industry A.I. Kraut & F.H. Freeman
(1992, Stock #152) $30.00

Using an Art Technique to Facilitate Leadership Development C. De Ciantis (1995, Stock #166) ... $30.00

Why Executives Lose Their Balance J.R. Kofodimos (1989, Stock #137) $20.00

Why Managers Have Trouble Empowering: A Theoretical Perspective Based on
Concepts of Adult Development W.H. Drath (1993, Stock #155) $15.00

SELECTED BOOKS:

Balancing Act: How Managers Can Integrate Successful Careers and Fulfilling Personal Lives
J.R. Kofodimos (1993, Stock #247) $27.00

Beyond Ambition: How Driven Managers Can Lead Better and Live Better R.E. Kaplan,
W.H. Drath, & J.R. Kofodimos (1991, Stock #227) $29.95

Breaking the Glass Ceiling: Can Women Reach the Top of America's Largest Corporations?
(Updated Edition) A.M. Morrison, R.P. White, & E. Van Velsor (1992, Stock #236A) $12.50

Choosing to Lead K.E. Clark & M.B. Clark (1994, Stock #249) $35.00

Developing Diversity in Organizations: A Digest of Selected Literature A.M. Morrison &
K.M. Crabtree (1992, Stock #317) $25.00

Discovering Creativity: Proceedings of the 1992 International Creativity and Innovation
Networking Conference S.S. Gryskiewicz (Ed.) (1993, Stock #319) $30.00

Executive Selection: A Look at What We Know and What We Need to Know
D.L. DeVries (1993, Stock #321) $20.00

Healing the Wounds: Overcoming the Trauma of Layoffs and Revitalizing Downsized
Organizations D.M. Noer (1993, Stock #245) $26.00

If I'm In Charge Here, Why Is Everybody Laughing? D.P. Campbell (1980, Stock #205) $9.40

If You Don't Know Where You're Going You'll Probably End Up Somewhere Else
D.P. Campbell (1974, Stock #203) $8.95

Inklings: Collected Columns on Leadership and Creativity D.P. Campbell (1992, Stock #233) $15.00

Leadership Education 1994-1995: A Source Book F.H. Freeman, K.B. Knott, &
M.K. Schwartz (Eds.) (1994, Stock #322) $59.00

Leadership: Enhancing the Lessons of Experience R.L. Hughes, R.C. Ginnett, & G.J. Curphy
(1992, Stock #246) $40.95

The Lessons of Experience: How Successful Executives Develop on the Job M.W. McCall, Jr.,
M.M. Lombardo, & A.M. Morrison (1988, Stock #211) $22.95

Making Diversity Happen: Controversies and Solutions A.M. Morrison, M.N. Ruderman, &
M. Hughes-James (1993, Stock #320) $25.00

Measures of Leadership K.E. Clark & M.B. Clark (Eds.) (1990, Stock #215) $59.50

The New Leaders: Guidelines on Leadership Diversity in America A.M. Morrison
(1992, Stock #238) $29.00

Readings in Innovation S.S. Gryskiewicz & D.A. Hills (Eds.) (1992, Stock #240) $25.00

Take the Road to Creativity and Get Off Your Dead End D.P. Campbell (1977, Stock #204) $8.95

Whatever It Takes: The Realities of Managerial Decision Making (Second Edition)
M.W. McCall, Jr., & R.E. Kaplan (1990, Stock #218) $30.40

The Working Leader: The Triumph of High Performance Over Conventional Management
Principles L.R. Sayles (1993, Stock #243) $24.95

SPECIAL PACKAGES:

Conversations with CEOs (includes 310 & 316) $16.00

Development & Derailment (includes 136, 138, & 144) $30.00

The Diversity Collection (includes 145, 236, 238, 317, & 320) $85.00

Executive Selection Package (includes 141, 321, & 157) $32.00

Feedback to Managers: Volumes I & II (includes 149 & 150) $85.00

Personal Growth, Taking Charge, and Enhancing Creativity (includes 203, 204, & 205) $20.00

Discounts are available. Please write for a comprehensive Publication & Products Catalog. Address
your request to: Publication, Center for Creative Leadership, P.O. Box 26300, Greensboro, NC
27438-6300, 910-545-2805, or fax to 910-545-3221. All prices subject to change.

ORDER FORM

Name _____ Title _____

Organization _____

Mailing Address _____
(street address required for mailing)

City/State/Zip _____

Telephone _____ FAX _____
(telephone number required for UPS mailing)

Quantity	Stock No.	Title	Unit Cost	Amount
		Subtotal		
		Shipping and Handling (add 6% of subtotal with a $4.00 minimum; add 40% on all international shipping)		
		NC residents add 6% sales tax; CA residents add 7% sales tax; CO residents add 6.2% sales tax		
		TOTAL		

METHOD OF PAYMENT

❏ Check or money order enclosed (payable to Center for Creative Leadership).

❏ Purchase Order No. _____ (Must be accompanied by this form.)

❏ Charge my order, plus shipping, to my credit card:
　　　❏ American Express　❏ Discover　❏ MasterCard　❏ VISA

ACCOUNT NUMBER:_____ EXPIRATION DATE: MO.___ YR.___

NAME OF ISSUING BANK: _____

SIGNATURE _____

❏ Please put me on your mailing list.
❏ Please send me the Center's quarterly newsletter, *Issues & Observations.*

Publication • Center for Creative Leadership • P.O. Box 26300
Greensboro, NC 27438-6300
910-545-2805 • FAX 910-545-3221

Client Priority Code: R

fold here

PLACE
STAMP
HERE

CENTER FOR CREATIVE LEADERSHIP
PUBLICATION
P.O. Box 26300
Greensboro, NC 27438-6300